ADVANCE PRAISE *for*
NIGHT WINGS

Sally Nelson illuminates the mysteries of the night world in this inspiring book by revealing how dreams bear an uncanny resemblance to the night hawk, which flies into the heart of darkness and returns to the day world with the kernel of wisdom needed for us to develop self-awareness. With a keen eye for the numinous dimension of dreams, Nelson encourages us to give dreams back their wings through the practice of writing them down and letting them fly into whatever form they demand, whether it be poetry, prose, or short stories. Her guidance will help analysts, clients, artists and dreamers, all who passionately believe in the healing power of dreams.

—PHIL COUSINEAU, author of
Once and Future Myths: The Power of Ancient Stories in Modern Times

This book will help the dreamer to write and the writer to dream. It embodies the maxim "research is me-search" and is a balance of objective and subjective material. I was moved by the author's openness and courage to share with others from her authentic self.

—DAVID H. ROSEN, M.D., author of
Transforming Depression: Healing the Soul Through Creativity
and *The Tao of Jung: The Way of Integrity*

Sally Nelson has done for dreams what Joseph Campbell did for myths. She has shown us the way to enter their wonders. *Night Wings* is a luminous guide to reflecting on our inner lives. The more we explore our dreams, the better we understand our mythic journeys.

—JONATHAN YOUNG, PH.D.,
Founding Curator, *Joseph Campbell Archives*

Teaching readers how to use their "dream themes" as springboards for constructing prose, poetry, or stories, Sally J. Nelson presents examples to strengthen the connection between dream experiences and creative expression. In the process of dream writing, Nelson hopes readers will learn about their inner worlds and establish a deep connection with their "dreaming soul." She includes Jungian concepts, transpersonal psychology, and holographic metaphors to familiarize readers with the ideas of earlier travelers upon these pathways. The writing style is delightfully fluid and admirably reflects the techniques outlined on each page. I have never read a book exactly like *Night Wings* and can envision it helping readers make a quantum leap in the development of their personal and professional writing styles.

—STANLEY KRIPPNER, PH.D.,
co-author of *Extraordinary Dreams and How to Work with Them.*

Gifted, passionate, a heroine's journey, Sally Nelson shows us how the *dream writer* can build a bridge spanning the dreamtime and visionary meditation to inspire creative writing. She teaches us to develop a relationship between the unconscious source of all creative imagination and practical, creative expression.

—ALBERTO VILLOLDO PH.D.,
author of *Shaman, Healer, Sage*

Sally Nelson offers a way of breathing life into our dreams, of appreciating and integrating the intelligence and guidance offered by these nightly treasures. Through her many fine writing exercises and examples she helps us become midwives for the birth of our own souls.

—VIC MANSFIELD, author of
Synchronicity, Science, and Soul-Making and
Head and Heart: A Personal Exploration of Science and the Sacred.

NIGHT WINGS

A Soulful Dreaming
and Writing Practice

SALLY J. NELSON

NICOLAS-HAYS, INC.
Berwick, Maine

For
Nav Tej
"New Light"
Dearest Daughter
Awesome Mentor
Beloved Friend

First published in 2004 by
Nicolas-Hays, Inc.
P. O. Box 1126
Berwick, ME 03901-1126
www.nicolashays.com

LIBRARY OF CONGRESS CATALOGING-IN-PUBLICATION DATA
Nelson, Sally J.
Night wings : a soulful dreaming and writing practice / Sally J. Nelson
1st American paperback edition
p. cm.
Includes bibliographical references and index.
ISBN 0-89254-088-5 (pbk. : alk. paper)
I. Dreams.   2. Creative writing—Psychological aspects.   I. Title
BF1091.N45 G78 2004
154.6'3--dc22   2004001095

Cover and text design by Kathryn Sky-Peck.
Typeset in 11/16 Centaur
Printed in the United States of America
10 09 08 07 06 05 04
7 6 5 4 3 2 1
VG
The paper used in this publication meets the minimum requirements of the American National
Standard for Information Sciences—Permanence of Paper for Printed Library Materials
Z39.48–1992 (R1997).

contents

exercises

acknowledgments

DEEPEST APPRECIATION to John A. Sanford, who introduced me to "The Kingdom Within"; Victor Daniels, Ph.D, who taught me to "put words around it"; Gordon Tappan, Ph.D., who showed me how to "see" both my inner and outer visions; Stanley Krippner, Ph.D., who taught me to track my dreams; and Katie Sanford, M.A., who helped me to find my own "position."

To my daughter Nav Tej, the light of my life; Brandon Wendell, who loves the light of my life; Don Isbell, who encouraged and believed in me; and Lizbeth Hamlin, who listened and cared.

To Stu Breisch, who loves, respects, and repeatedly asks me, "What is reality?" Joan Winchell listened with love and formed our supportive writing group: Karen Winston, Kathi Olsen, Joan Murphy, and Anne Reich. Jan Freya encouraged and helped my writing.

To my dear Jung friends: Sandy Sanford, Jack and Linny Sanford, Ron Strange, and all who pass through that inner door in search of the beyond.

introduction

Night Wings is inspired by a lifetime of dreaming and writing, more than thirty years of exploring dreams with my clients, and a combination of events in my life that began with a series of dreams. These dreams foreshadowed and then conveyed the death of a loved one to me at the exact time of his death.

About a year later, Karen Winston, one of the women in my writing group wrote a stirring vignette. The images were vivid and they seemed different from other things she had written. I commented that the story had a dreamlike quality. She responded, "Well, as a matter of fact, I was remembering a dream I had last night as I was writing." She said the dream had been so lifelike that, even though she had written it in her dream journal, it had lingered in her mind all morning. She said the dream seemed to push her to write it again and let her imagination play with it.

I said, "Wouldn't it be wonderful if we could access the place where our dreams are created when we are writing?" All the women in the group exclaimed, "Yes!" We talked about how frustrating it can be to become aware of a vivid dream and then feel it fade as we wake up. We connected that feeling with the frustration of having the urge to write, but being unable to drop down to the source of our imagination. We all agreed it would be very satisfying if we could go there, to that dream place, and tap that source of creativity when we are awake and feeling the desire to write. I left our writing group that day musing about the idea of tapping the source of dreams for creative writing.

Soon after that meeting, Dr. Stanley Krippner, one of my first and most influential dream mentors, came to speak to the San Diego Friends of Jung about dreams and personal mythology. As I listened to his familiar voice and his encouragement to continue to follow my dreams, I suddenly realized that dreams *are* the path to creative imagination! Duh! In that moment, the discussion with my writing group and my many years of dream writing synthesized into the idea for this book.

Another powerful catalytic experience that reinforced my decision to write *Night Wings* happened when I met Michael Quirke, a wood carver and storyteller in Sligo, Ireland. Michael's shop window was full of fascinating wooden carvings of mythological Celtic heroes and heroines. One in particular caught my eye and drew me inside the shop. I took the figure out of the window and studied it closely. As I turned to the artist, he took the carving from me and held it in his large, capable hands. He ran his fingertips down the body of what, at first glance, seemed to be a woman encased in a feathered cape. He stroked its hooded head. The hood surrounded a heart-shaped black hollow where I expected to see a face. The figure held an indistinct object cupped between her hands.

Curious about the carving, I looked more closely. Embedded in what looked like a hood draped around the top of the figure's head were two piercing eyes that stared back at me. I pulled back and peered into the dark cavity beneath the eyes. I suddenly recognized the gaping mouth of a fierce bird of prey. A needle-sharp beak helped to form the black, heart-shaped void. Below that black, hollow, heart-face, human arms and hands emerged from the edges of two magnificent, mighty wings that folded around this mystically intriguing creature's body. Below the elongated wings, two clawed feet with almost-human toes gripped the base of the figure. The figure seemed to morph and transform. The nighthawk began to spread her imposing spectral wings. I have no doubt that I heard her great wings begin to flap and her cawing screeches pierce the evening light as she prepared to take flight.

The artist smiled. "Ah, now this one is the night hawk," he drawled in his Irish brogue. "This is not a hero from the Celtic myths, like my other carvings. I made this one up. It represents something important about the Celts. You see, the Celts took their dreams quite seriously. The title of this carving is *Where Is Wisdom to be Found?* According to the Irish File (poet-seer), he explained, the answer is "by looking within." "The dreamer, like the night hawk," he continued, "flies into the heart of darkness, into the aisling (the dream vision), seizes the nut of wisdom, and exits with the dream intact." He pointed to the object, shaped like a nut, held between the hands of the carved figure. "This is the kernel of wisdom."

Michael's story about his carving intrigued me. I love synchronistic events. They give me the opportunity to witness the existence of the divine. The carving and his story together created a perfect metaphor for what the dreamer must do to begin a soulful dream-writing practice. I brought the figure home with me and named her Night Wings. This sacred winged being has perched on my writing desk ever since, flying into my dreams and my imagination to retrieve the kernels of wisdom that have informed my writing. She helps me to take flight on my own night wings, into my dream visions to the places where wisdom is found. She inspires me to describe my dream experiences and to return to outer reality with the kernels of wisdom and the treasures that are hard to find, but well worth seeking. She encourages me to use these kernels and treasures to cultivate my spiritual awareness and my mindful creativity.

As I began to rough out the connection between following dreams and creative writing, I consulted the *Collected Works of C. G. Jung*. I came across the quote that introduces the first chapter of this book and inspired its title. Jung validated the importance of dreams by studying more than 80,000 of them in the course of his practice as a psychotherapist. His research and clinical experience support the significance of dreams and the unconscious psyche to individual and collective evolution. Jung realized that, in addition to guiding you to heal, dreams are inner experiences that parallel your outer life and step ahead of your conscious awareness to guide you to actualize your potential.

Night Wings is more than a book about how to write your dreams. It is also about the ways in which your dreams inform your life and your creative writing, and about how your life, in turn, informs your dreams. It is a guide to help you develop writing skills and extend your dream themes into prose, poetry, and stories. The examples and exercises presented here will help you strengthen the connection between your dream experiences and your creative expression.

Dream writing is a conceptual, meditative, and experiential practice that weaves together a psychological, emotional, and spiritual method of dream exploration that inspires creative writing. As you write your dreams and visionary meditations, you also learn how your psyche functions and informs you through your dreams. You can flesh out your dreams by using examples and exercises that guide you through a process of dream exploration and creative writing.

This writing practice offers you an opportunity to step outside of your conditioned reality and fly on your own night wings into your inner universe of unlimited possibilities. In the process, you go beyond the concepts of how your psyche functions and develop and experience a relationship with your dreaming soul, the source of your dreams. That relationship increases your confidence and your ability to consult your inner wisdom. Those consultations can inform your ability to make clear decisions in your life and inspire your creative writing.

You will be challenged to journey into the depths of your psyche to bring what you find into your life though creative writing. Your dreams provide you with metaphors that reflect your personal, collective, and transpersonal development. In the process of writing and reflecting on these dreams, you recognize and change patterns of thinking, feeling, and behavior that are no longer useful. You strengthen your sense of personal authenticity and identity as you enhance your psychological and spiritual awareness through the process of soulful dreaming and creative writing.

Writing your dreams, visionary meditations, prose, and poetry is a creative healing process that opens you to the inner source of your creative imagination. Dreams are often the visions that foreshadow outer life events and promote ongoing growth and individuation. The messages of dreams are a type of oracle based on your own inner wisdom rather than the wisdom of others.

As you expand, extend, and fly on your own creative imaginal night wings, you are asking your dreaming soul: Where is wisdom to be found? All the sages say: "Within." When you make a commitment to be 100 percent present in the moment of your dreaming, your visionary meditation, and your writing, you are enriched and enlightened by those experiences. Your dreaming soul asks no less of you than a friend or lover. It desires dialogue, attention, and energy. It asks for time, love, courage, and authentic engagement.

Dream writing is a way to bring your inner wisdom into your life. Over time, you learn to understand and trust the messages your dreams bring. These messages can guide you to find your authentic position in life. The benefits you gain from allowing your dreams to inform your choices assure you that you can always turn to your dreams as a resource for trustworthy ongoing guidance. In turn, you find that your outer life experiences come into alignment with your inner dreams in a powerful way.

1

the
dreaming
psyche

What if there were a living agency beyond our everyday human world . . .
[and] a door that opens upon that human world from a world beyond,
allowing unknown and mysterious powers to act upon man and carry
him on the wings of the night to a more personal destiny?

—C. G. JUNG, *CW* 15, ¶ 148

Each time you fall asleep, you have an opportunity to stretch your imaginal night wings and fly from your outer conscious reality into the mysterious realm of your inner unconscious reality. Your dreams are metaphorical stories that help you discover the purpose of your life and teach you how to walk the path of your soul's becoming.

Dreams from your personal unconscious reveal the ways in which your ego is or is not in control of your conscious life. Dreams from your collective unconscious reveal your relationship to the history of human experience. Dreams from your transpersonal unconscious unveil the path your soul is meant to travel.

SACRED SPACE

Dreams occur in a place, space, and time beyond ordinary reality that I consider sacred. When you encounter the mysteries and treasures of your dreams, you enter dimensions of nonordinary reality that exist beyond linear time and space where anything is possible. You may encounter numinous (emotionally and spiritually gripping) dreams that lead you to a reservoir of creative energy in your unconscious psyche. You give form to that energy through your unique voice and style of creative expression.

Some people can enter this sacred space without going to sleep and dreaming. They call it the "zone" of creative imagination and inspiration. Other people experience sacred space only when they are asleep or have invoked an altered state of awareness like a reverie, a trance, or a deep meditative state. The dream-writing practice described here asks you to open yourself to experience the nonlinear and parallel realities of the sacred space of your dreams and to pay attention to what you encounter.

For Carl Jung, the mystery beyond waking reality is the personal and collective transpersonal unconscious. For the Buddha, beyond is the infinite ocean of being. The Australian aborigines travel beyond ordinary time in the mystifying realm of dreamtime. For the shaman, the dreaming experience is the warrior's path of the heart, which leads beyond the literal experience of personal wounds and the fear of death into transpersonal transcendent experiences. All transpersonal and religious traditions acknowledge that there is some creative force, some form of energy that is not accounted for by the personal ego of the individual or of collective humanity.

PSYCHIC ENERGY

Dreams are an alchemical amalgamation of various elements of psychic energy. Those elements combine in the human psyche to form something that can be imagined as holographic images. Those images contain information, perceptions, and experiences that lie both within and beyond your apprehension or the grasp of your intellect.

Each psyche is a complex molecular structure that has a vibratory resonance that receives and transmits invisible energy. This psychic energy fuels consciousness and unconsciousness, and affects and informs the various functions of your psyche. The patterns of that energy come to you and are expressed by you in obvious forms such as images, thoughts, and emotions, but they also exist in more subtle forms that you can learn to recognize. These subtle forms of essential energy are usually referred to as metaphysical, soulful, spiritual, and transcendental experiences.

Your dreaming soul, or what Jung refers to as the Self, is like an internal operator of your psyche. It is the instinctual, intuitive source of essential energy that activates your creative imagination. It is the origin of what Jung calls the collective transpersonal unconscious.

Your conscious ego is like an external operator of your psyche, the part that deals with outer reality. What is reality? Much of your outer reality is a result of what you believe it to be and, therefore, what you create it to be. Moreover, what you believe is learned and conditioned through conventional cultural guidelines. Your reality is limited and contained in the proverbial black box unless you question what you have collected in that box. You can change your reality by changing your beliefs about reality. You change your beliefs by broadening your inner and outer experiences. One way to broaden your perception of inner reality is to court intentional communication with your dreaming soul.

A JUNGIAN MODEL OF THE PSYCHE

Try to visualize the functions of your psyche as layers inside the form of a pyramid. Your conscious ego rests at the top like the eye at the top of the pyramid on a one-dollar bill. Your personal unconscious in the middle interfaces with the collective and then the transpersonal unconscious at the bottom of the pyramid. Picture your conscious personal ego resting upon and being informed by a broad and deep foundation of genetic and universal contents. Thus Jungian psychology is known as "depth" psychology.[1]

Your Personal Unconscious

The personal unconscious just beneath the surface of your awake, conscious ego is the top level of your unconscious. It contains the literal and symbolic memories, images, and sensations from everything that you have ever seen, heard, touched, tasted, and smelled, along with all your thoughts, emotions, and beliefs about those experiences. All the positive and negative experiences of this lifetime are stored in your personal unconscious in a form that can be imagined as three-dimensional holographic images. These images are based on memories and fueled or kept alive by psychic energy. When these memories are positive and enlightening, their psychic energy supports creative development. When they are confusing or painful, they can subvert creative development. Then, psychic energy is constricted and trapped in your personal unconscious as painful repressed memories.

Personal dreams are composed from the memories and experiences stored in your personal unconscious. They are also informed by your collective and transpersonal unconscious, which encompasses human evolution and everything known or unknown to you that informs that evolution. Thus, personal dreams contain what is necessary for your personal evolution. You receive power in the form of psychic energy from such dreams. In order to integrate and be able to direct that power, you must give tangible form to the dream.

You transform the energy from a personal dream into useable awareness when you recognize the literal and personal nature and message of the dream. You can recognize the personal contents of dreams as having their source in your personal past through characters, settings, or themes that are familiar to you. Sometimes what is familiar is pleasant, and sometimes it is not.

Meet Your Shadow

When you explore experiences and images in dreams, they often shape-shift and take on other forms. You can follow their development over a series of dreams. You meet personal shadow aspects of your self as characters in dreams whom you do not like, as well as ones you hold in exceptionally high esteem. These shadow characters may appear as people you actually know, or not. They are all aspects of your unconscious that present the undiscovered positive potentials that you do not yet recognize, and negative potentials you prefer to ignore.

These potentials are usually projected onto other people. Shadow elements, hidden in the recesses of your psyche, are like holograms that you project out of your unconscious. They take form on and around other people and seem, at the time, to be part of the other person. You don't usually realize you are imagining and projecting aspects of your own potentials onto other people. Projection is a difficult concept to understand. It is even more challenging to become conscious of when you are projecting.

I realize that I am projecting when I have an intense positive or negative emotional reaction to a person or situation. I have learned to realize, and therefore trust, that most of the intensity I feel in response to another person's behavior is about my own unrecognized positive or negative potential to behave in similar ways. When my reactions to others are intense, I usually do not recognize or admit that I have those same characteristics myself. That is why I'm so emotionally impacted by the other person. To complicate the matter even more, it is also true that the "other" upon whom I cast my projection probably does have some of the characteristics that trigger my reaction.

Jung says, "Projections change the world into the replica of one's own unknown face."[2] The best way to sort this out is to remember that, even if you think another person is a creep, when your reaction is intense, you are no longer objective about how creepy they actually are. You have added the intensity of your own unconscious creepiness to the situation. When you are aware of the same characteristics in yourself, your response is less intense and you are more able to accept that person's creepiness with compassion.

Personal shadow characteristics tend to appear in dreams as characters of the same gender as the dreamer. Since I know that I usually project my shadow characteristics onto others, the natures of those characters in my dreams help me become more conscious of the nature of my projections. I'm always tempted when I first review a dream to think automatically that the dream is about the characters in the dream. If the Dali Lama or Guru Maya shows up in a dream, I usually think the dream is about them, until I remind myself that, most of the time, the characters are standing in for aspects of myself that I don't recognize or that I reject. As you learn to understand the dream shadow characters as aspects of yourself, you reclaim the psychic energy they hold captive. As you recognize and accept your positive and your negative qualities, you become more authentic. We will explore more about the shadow as we delve deeper into this writing practice.

The Collective Transpersonal Unconscious

Jung characterizes the unconscious as transcending and surrounding the conscious mind.[3] However, for the sake of consistency, picture the collective and transpersonal layers of your unconscious psyche as lying beneath and beyond your personal unconscious. Imagine those layers as a vast Milky Way of essential psychic energy that mythically extends into "that cosmic night which was psyche long before there was any ego consciousness and which will remain psyche no matter how far our ego consciousness extends."[4]

Within that vastness, there is a limitless expanse of possibility out of which the beliefs, behaviors, and myths of all human cultures evolve. Your dreaming soul reflects upon these encoded memories of genetic and evolutionary human experiences that have taken place over millennia. These etched memories inform the archetypal images, characters, and experiences that make up your dreams, your imagination, and your spiritual and outer life experiences. The images and the experiences you create in your life emerge and take form out of the matrix of essential psychic energy that is your personal, collective, and transpersonal unconscious.

Meet the Archetypes

The archetypes you meet in your dreams are your psyche's versions of some of the basic constellations of collective and transpersonal experiences of humanity. They are the visions through which your dreaming soul connects you to your basic instincts and cosmic realities. Like blueprints that reflect the make-up of your collective and transpersonal psyche, they represent the way you have assimilated core experiences through memory traces of your relationship to your genetic and collective human history.

Such archetypal images appear in the dreams and experiences of people in all eras and cultures. They are found in ancient myths, and in modern novels, and movies. They appear in dreams and in human dramas. They are heroes and heroines, victims and fools. They appear as gods and goddesses, devils and angels. They are saints and sinners. They are your allies and your enemies. They may appear as people, animals, acts of nature, bursts of energy, or entities with a metaphysical or spiritual presence. Archetypes are independent, dominating, and

Archetypes

autonomous dream characters. They appear in dreams as primal forces with a potent impact that reverberates through your psyche.

These powerful beings and experiences inhabit your unconscious psyche and influence your thoughts, feelings, and behaviors. You are not usually aware of that influence until you begin to discover them in your dreams. When they show up in my dreams, I feel them so deeply that I have no doubt they are real entities and I know they are influencing my outer reality. I have a healthy respect for their power and I am always curious about their purpose.

The characters in your dreams are representations of aspects of your personal, collective, and transpersonal history. Transpersonal archetypes are thought by some metaphysicians to be remnant etchings of past lives. However you define them, these characters can enlighten and transform your awareness, encourage your individuation process, and transform your life. Dream writing gives you the opportunity to encounter and learn from the archetypes that reverberate and constellate in your unconscious psyche. As you dream and write, you develop a sense of the nature of the facets of your psyche that inform your ego and your dreaming soul.

Your Ego and Your Dreaming Soul

Like the fiery eye of the sun, your awake-and-aware ego shines a clear intense light upon your personal, literal, and outer life path. Your conscious ego travels along the linear roads of awareness and experience. As you observe and attempt to understand everything you experience, your aware ego continues to track its intended course. Linear time, as your ego knows time, flies. The daylight realm offers it an ongoing source of discovery and the opportunity to master new experiences. Most of the time, your conscious ego is concerned with helping you survive and thrive in the outer world. It is busy sorting, ordering, controlling, and making sense of daily life.

Like the setting sun, your awake ego sets into sleep. When you sleep and dream, or when you enter a nonordinary state of awareness such as a daydream, trance, reverie, or meditation, your conscious ego is no longer in complete control. You turn your attention away from your literal personal experiences and enter a more mysterious and mythical transpersonal reality.

Just as the glaring eye of the sun is eclipsed by the luminous eye of the moon, your penetrating conscious ego is eclipsed by the softer gaze of your dreaming soul. As the daytime landscape becomes lost in darkness, your dreaming soul shines a more diffuse light upon the seascape of your inner world. That light shines into and beyond the realm of your personal psyche. It is a soft light that shimmers across the surface of your unconscious sea and glimmers into your depths. Your dreaming soul wanders in a cosmic ocean-like realm of unconscious imagination and reverie. As it meanders along this less intentional path, a less familiar kind of life begins to stir.

Here, in your unconscious psyche, your dreaming soul travels in a domain of nonlinear adventure, a realm of mythic imagination. Your dreaming soul is the source of your imagination and creativity. Each time you allow your ego to shift in the service of this inner journey, you strengthen the connection between your conscious ego and your unconscious self. As this bridge becomes reliable, your dreams respond and metaphorically reflect the underlying patterns in your personal and transpersonal character. Sometimes, your dreams reflect your place and your purpose in the larger composite pattern of collective human experience.

The more involved you are with your dream experiences, the more likely you are to meet both the egotistical and spiritual aspects of yourself. I have learned that my dreaming soul is a wise spiritual aspect of my psyche that will not be controlled by my ego. When I respect that spirit, it responds with gifts of discovery and wisdom. If I attempt to exploit that spirit in order to feel that I am special because of those gifts, it pulls the rug out from under my egotistical self-absorbed motives and I plunge into forgetful darkness.

My own dream-writing practice has definitely honed my conscious ego to become less personally absorbed and more able to work in partnership with my dreaming soul. I find that my motivations continue to become less self-serving and more in the service of helping my higher Self develop my creative potential so that I may contribute something meaningful to others.

Meet Your Dreaming Soul and Your Self

I use the term "dreaming soul" to designate an aspect of the archetype that Jung refers to as the Self, or the God within each of us. This Self, or dreaming soul, is the prototype for the element within human nature that promotes the evolution of life, consciousness, and individuation. It influences all levels of your psyche and guides you toward reaching your potential.

Your dreaming soul creates dreams that can guide you to heal when you need to and to discover and express your unique creative potential. Although a dream character that represents your higher Self may appear as a wise counselor or benevolent angel, it may just as well appear in the form of a trickster or a shadow daemon. In the past, I avoided mentors that came to me in a dream in an uncomfortable form by ignoring or forgetting the dream. However, I have learned that doesn't work. Those pesky, unpleasant images and characters return until I make myself write the dream, even though I would rather ignore it because I don't like it. My individuation and evolution require me to acknowledge both the dark and the light aspects of my shadow.

For instance, the other night I had a dream that my brother, who is dead, called me on the phone and said, "We need you." I was busy in the dream, starting a new program of learning, and didn't want to be interrupted. He insisted, "We need you." I ignored the dream all day, but it kept niggling at me. That evening, I called my mother. She said she was failing. She described her sensations to me and I felt sure she was having mini strokes and/or heart failure. She was unwilling to go to the hospital until I told her about the dream. Then she agreed to go. I reflected on the dream, not only as a nudge to check in on my mother, but as a call to reflect upon the challenge of how to stay on my path when people I care about need my time and attention.

The Self speaks to you through your dreaming soul. It communicates something about how your ego is controlling your attitudes and the situations and relationships in your life. When you seek guidance from your dreaming soul and listen to your dreams, you are given the gift of your own genuine truth. It may contradict or compensate for what you believe your truth to be. That's when things get interesting. It is your responsibility to understand your inner truth and embody it in your life. When you contact your authentic Self and express what you experience, you initiate and engage in an ongoing process of personal and transpersonal change and evolution. "The Self does not become conscious by itself," Jung tells us, "but has always been taught . . . through a tradition of knowing."[5]

INDIVIDUATION AND
TRANSPERSONAL INSIGHT

The goal of individuation, simply stated, is to develop and manifest your full potential. From a transpersonal point of view, consciousness is the central dimension and essence of human experience. The psyche contains a spectrum of states of consciousness that range from ordinary ego awareness, to nonordinary states that are free of the usual limitations and distortions caused by social conditioning. Transpersonal insight is characterized by awareness that goes beyond the intellect and emotions of the personal ego to the essential energy that some call spirit, which creates and nourishes all existence.

The transpersonal perspective of the psyche contrasts with traditional Western psychology, which gives primary authority to the ego. I took a less traditional path within Western psychology when I chose to include working with dreams as a significant part of my work. I slowly developed this dream-writing practice as a way to experience and flesh out the creatures that live in the depths of my psyche and to help my clients do the same. These creatures appear in my dreams—and in theirs, and in yours—as images from the depths beyond the ego. They are fashioned by the ancient and wise dreaming soul. As I discovered, experienced, and related to the archetypal creatures that appeared in dreams, I recognized them as the heralds of personal and transpersonal growth.

Once I committed myself to this relationship with my dreaming soul, there was no turning back. If I ignored my dreams by not giving them form, I found out that the creatures that were capable of befriending me were equally capable of erupting in nightmares, outer conflicts, and physical, emotional, and mental suffering. When I suffered this way, I exhausted my creative energy by using it to battle the beasts within and the seeming enemies that appeared in my outer experiences.

I learned to assimilate the energy of my nightmarish dreams by returning to dream writing. The dreaming soul, like any beloved one, does not appreciate being ignored. When I returned my attention to my dreams, I felt connected with a wellspring of vital energy. My suffering became curiosity, and curiosity led to creativity.

Although my dreams reserved the right to be nightmarish when necessary, when I was tending them, they had a different quality. They did not engender panic. They invited my curiosity. I experienced them as teaching me, rather than as poking, prodding, and scaring me. Joe Henderson, a Jungian analyst, once told me "When you point yourself in the right direction, the universe will line up to support you." Dream writing is a way to point your self in the right direction. It can be a sacred practice and, as such, deserves to be entered into with respect and commitment.

As I continued my dream-writing practice and research, I recognized that people who tend to their dreams as a way of expanding their reality are similar in some ways to ancient people. Like shamans, gurus, and prophets, they tend to be intentional, autonomous, and creative, and to have an animated, playful sense of humor. Despite their focus on nonlinear reality, they tend to be reality-oriented and good problem solvers. They also tend to be calm and centered, and to accept themselves and others. Many of them have numinous experiences that transcend ordinary reality. They recognize such numinous experiences when they appear in dreams.

Numinous Experience

Numinous dreams can be visionary, prescient, spiritual, or metaphysical. I have learned through my own experience, and from reading and studying Western psychologists like Jung, spiritual leaders like Christ and Buddha, and Hindu, Tibetan, Zen, Judaic, shamanic, and pagan spiritual traditions, that numinous, highly charged experiences become possible through contemplative practices. These practices include dream exploration, prayer, meditation, wilderness experiences, and other ceremonial ways of altering awareness in order to more directly experience the essential vital energy of the universal life force.

People who develop a transpersonal perspective often report that they have had mystical or ego-transcending experiences. During these experiences, they suddenly feel a powerful transcendental or extrasensory state of consciousness. They experience heightened clarity, insight, and appreciation of the integrated nature of the universe and their unity with it. Such experiences may include an indescribable altered sense of space and time, such as often occurs in dream-time-space. These transcendent, numinous experiences activate the potential for healing and creative expression. Highly charged numinous experiences like these are life-enhancing for people who are psychologically healthy. They tend to produce long-lasting benefits in terms of increased awareness and a sense of well-being. Such experiences have been described in many cultures and in various periods of time. They have been called mystical, transcendental, cosmic, alchemical, and shamanic.

My numinous dream experiences have helped me trust my self and integrate contradictory elements in my life. They have increased my capacity to appreciate the inexplicable yet undeniable source that has brought the universe and all life into being. Whether I call that source Goddess, God, a higher power, the wonder of subatomic physics, chaos theory, morphic resonance, or creativity, it is an energy that I recognize and can feel. What I feel is nonordinary. It is extraordinary.

Extraordinary Awareness

The dream-writing practice presented here is one of a variety of powerful ways to investigate extraordinary awareness. You have the possibility of shifting out of ordinary reality and journeying through and beyond your personal experiences to widen and deepen the scope of your awareness. You can expand your capacity for insight, understanding, compassion, and creative expression. The dream language of images and feelings originates in your passive imagination—passive because you do not create your dreams by your conscious intention. The stuff of your dreams lies sleeping in your unconscious psyche until you begin to track your dreams and express them in some form. In the process of giving them form through self-reflection, meditation, and writing, you exercise and increase your physical, emotional, mental, and spiritual energy.

THE POWER OF REFLECTION
AND VISIONARY MEDITATION

Reflecting on dreams is a form of meditation that develops your ability to observe and give form to the images and messages they give to you. Rather than noticing them and then letting them pass by as you do in mindfulness meditation, you guide and focus your mind so you can interact with your dreams through writing. The writing centers you and nurtures your creative and spiritual development. It aligns you with your unconscious potential.

You are most able to encounter your dreaming soul when you center and focus your attention and your intention. When you are calm and alert, you are better able to concentrate on what you experience as you write. To do this, you must stop focusing on outside distractions and turn instead to your inner experiences. As you withdraw your attention from the stimulation of the outer world, you experience a physical, emotional, and mental change of awareness that supports your intention to attend to your inside world of sensations, emotions, ideas, and images.

You can use almost any form of meditation, relaxation, or trance induction to become centered, calm, and alert as a preparation for dreaming and writing. Try Exercise 1 if you do not have a method to center yourself. It is a simple form of meditation that can be used to focus your awareness as you continue to develop your talent for dreaming, healing, individuation, and creative writing.

Each of us can choose to claim the possibility of fulfilling our creative potential. For you to do so, you may find that writing your dreams leads you backward toward what is necessary for healing, or forward toward new discoveries. Your journey toward individuation is a lifelong process of integrating the many facets of potential available in your psyche. Your individuation, the process of developing into a fully differentiated, balanced and unified person, is the way in which you cultivate a partnership between your conscious ego and your unconscious psyche. This partnership will activate the psychic energy that fuels your creative impulse.

Psychic energy is expressed biologically, psychologically, spiritually, and creatively in your life and in the situations and characters in your dreams. From a biological point of view, it flows through the central and autonomic nervous systems. In the Chinese philosophy of the Tao, this energy is called *chi*. In the Hindu philosophy of Tantra, it is known as *kundalini*. In the shamanic tradition of Peru, it is found in the energy centers of the body, the *ojos de luce*, that correspond closely to the *chakra* centers of Tibetan Buddhism. In the symbolism of medieval alchemy, psychic energy is generated by the fusion of conscious and unconscious functions. Psychologically, psychic energy is generated by the challenges and triumphs of life. The focus of awareness on dreams and their transformation into conscious awareness increases the psychic energy that infuses and activates both ego consciousness and the unconscious psyche.

Your habitual patterns of thinking and acting influence the quality of your psychic energy and the quality of your psychic energy influences those patterns. When you intentionally repeat experiences that encourage personal healing and creative development, you change ineffective habitual patterns, invigorate your psychic energy, and stimulate your creative urge. That urge is a force that can determine the way you live your life, the way you die, and, as some believe, the way you are reborn in this life or beyond.

Therefore, it is worthwhile to pursue opportunities to heighten and refine your psychic and creative energy. Dream writing is one way to explore and influence the state of your psychic energy by giving it an intentional form. The more you experience your dreaming psyche, the more you increase your access to your psychic energy. Dream exploration expands your capacity and ability for personal healing and creative expression.

Healing and Creative Potential

The questions to ask about a dream are simple: What is the purpose of the dream? What effect is it meant to have? Dreams are inspirational experiences that act as a medium between the visible and invisible world for purposes of healing and expressing creative potential. Dreams stimulate imagination and the ability to digest and assimilate painful memories. They help touch and resolve negative emotional and mental patterns that may be blocking creative expression. To remember, record, and work with dreams is to become better prepared to digest life experiences and use them for healing and crafting the future.

Dream writing gives you an opportunity to discover what you do not yet know about yourself. What you discover helps you heal your emotional wounds and live a more harmonious life. When you keep an ongoing journal of your dreams, you flesh out the patterns of your woundedness and your healing. The process of healing transforms the energy caught in the emotional wound into creative energy.

This opportunity for healing is why dream writing usually begins with exploring dreams that are about your personal life as a way of healing and decreasing pain and conflict. The healing that occurs through dream writing is gradual and subtle, but it is profound. It exponentially increases your creativity, because it helps you resolve emotional ambivalence.

As you learn to recognize the symbolic meaning of your dreams, they guide you toward healthy ego development and self-esteem. When you continue working with your dreams through visionary meditation, you experience even more of their transformative power.

As healing progresses, your dreams become less dominated by personal issues and begin to offer you a wider, deeper, more evolutionary perception of human experience. Personal insight and this wider, deeper perception can inspire your creative writing as it has inspired countless authors, artists, scientists, and philosophers.

2

the
soulful source
of dreams

We must recognize that nothing is more difficult to bear with than oneself.
Yet even this most difficult of achievements becomes possible if we can
distinguish ourselves from the unconscious contents.

—C. G. JUNG, *CW* 7, ¶ 373

Most of your dream stories are reflections of your life. They echo your private thoughts, feelings, and behaviors, and the dynamics of your personal relationships. Other dreams may focus on the ways in which you are involved with your collective social environment. They may reflect your immediate social situations or those of the larger human collective. Still other dreams may focus on spiritual or transpersonal experiences that reflect the dynamics of how you are or are not aware of experiences that are not controlled by your ego.

The source of all of your dreams is your conscious and unconscious memories and the "entire psychic structure developed both upwards and downwards by [your] ancestors, in the course of the ages."[1] Dreams are like mysteries that you get to explore and attempt to solve. You will not solve them all, and that isn't even necessary for you to benefit from putting them in writing. The act of dreaming, even when you don't work with the dream, is beneficial. However, just as research has shown that writing about traumatic experiences can lead to resolution and healing, writing dreams can assist you to heal and externalize your creative potential. The benefits increase with additional reflection and writing.

There are several types of dreams and various ways to shed light on them. Their emotional intensity, images, setting, themes, and characters uniquely reflect your psyche. One way to gain perspective on a dream is to wonder what kind of dream it is. You may find that certain types of dreams tend to predominate for you. Although it is important to approach each dream as a unique metaphor, it can be helpful to begin with a sense of the level and type of dream you are exploring. Personal, collective, or transpersonal dreams may be traumatic, compensatory, prospective, telepathic, or precognitive in their form.

PERSONAL AND COLLECTIVE DREAMS

Personal dreams are based on life experiences that are stored as memories in your personal unconscious. They contain all the positive and negative experiences you have had from the moment of your birth (and, perhaps, before) to the moment of your dream (and, perhaps, beyond). Some reflect experiences from the distant past; others reflect current experiences; still others foreshadow the future. Some are combinations of all three. Personal dreams present symbols, metaphors, and mythic stories that help you become aware of emotional patterns that are active at the time of the dream. As you become familiar with those patterns and gain insight into them, you are better able to change them.

Some collective dreams are based on your relationship with people and your immediate world. They reflect the positive and negative experiences you have had within groups such as your family and school and work. Although they echo memory traces that are deeper in your unconscious, they are still closer to your personal unconscious. When they reflect the ancestral preconditions that influence your fate as an individual, they echo deeper memory traces that are genetic.[2]

Participating in dream analysis with a qualified therapist is the traditional way to begin personal dream exploration. I worked with Jungian analyst Katie Sanford for years. She is a gifted dream mentor who guided me to go deeper into my dreams to understand the cryptic language and vivid images they presented. She taught me to go beyond superficial, "obvious" interpretations and seek the symbolic meaning of my dreams. This is not easy. Our interactive process deeply enriched my dream work and taught me how to attend to my dreams subjectively, in terms of what they suggest about my inner development, and objectively, in terms of what they suggest about situations in my outer world. I have found, as have many of my clients and colleagues, that dream exploration is valuable both with and without professional consultation. Gaining insight into dreams requires commitment. It requires the curiosity, courage, and strength to explore the emotional experience and relate to the symbols and metaphors the dream uses to communicate its message.

It is sometimes difficult to recognize the symbols in your own dreams. However, dream writing can help you to develop an objective ability to sense the meaning of the symbols in your dreams. Over time, certain symbols and metaphors repeat. The process of writing them and your associations to them brings ever-increasing insight and understanding.

TRAUMATIC DREAMS

Traumatic dreams are a reaction to an outer situation that was emotionally devastating and/or life-threatening. They reflect an experience that caused extreme physical, emotional, or mental pain. Experiences such as emotional and/or physical abuse, torture, rape, war, terrorist attacks, natural disasters, accidents, death of a loved one, or severe injury to one's self or to a loved one all tend to produce recurring dreams that relive the traumatic event. Such dreams are not completely relieved by understanding them. They decrease in frequency, and eventually stop, only when the experience has been assimilated and the emotional shock of the event has lessened.

Jung refers to the trauma of military experience to express the power of traumatic dreams. "Psychiatrists considered . . . that a man should be pulled out of the front lines [when he dreamed] too much of war scenes, [because then] he no longer possessed any psychic defenses against the impressions from outside."[3]

COMPENSATORY DREAMS

According to Jung, a compensatory dream means that "the unconscious . . . adds to the conscious situation all those elements . . . which remained subliminal because of repression or because they were too feeble to reach consciousness."[4] This purposive compensation for the conscious outer situation of the dreamer is determined by his or her psychic nature. If you have a melancholy nature and are capable of responding to optimistic dreams, the compensation may come in an encouraging form. If you are not capable of responding to cheerful dreams, the compensation may come in a homeopathic way and may be even more despondent than your conscious attitude.

In many cases, a dream suggests what is needed for additional development by dramatizing an attitude or action that is not working. This type of dream helps you focus on a particular type of experience so you can become more aware of it and reflect on how you are living it. It may compensate or embellish your conscious attitudes or behaviors by either opposing or confirming them. If it does not vary much from the outer situation, it may be a confirmation that your conscious attitude is adequate.

A dream may compensate for a confused, conscious attitude by answering a question about something that is worrying you. It can either confirm or relieve anxiety. There are no absolute rules that apply to the purpose of a dream, but there are themes that recur in terms of how your dreams speak to you. In time, you recognize the style in which the language of your dreams communicates with you. Maya Angelou describes a type of dream that relieves anxiety by letting her know when her writing is going well: "There is a dream . . . it means . . . that the work is going well . . . I get that dream [and] I know the work is going to be all right."[5]

REDUCTIVE COMPENSATORY DREAMS

When you are inflated—"full of yourself"—a reductive dream compensates with a metaphor that devalues or destroys your conscious position. You may be successful in the outer world, but may not have grown inwardly to the level of what Jung calls your "outward immanence." In these circumstances, Jung points out, "a reduction or devaluation is . . . a compensatory effort at self-regulation."[6]

When a dream takes a view that opposes, or even demolishes, your conscious view, its intention is to prod you to reconsider your position and consider other options. A dream will exaggerate an outer situation and your attitude about the situation when you are caught in feelings of inflation or self-aggrandizement. It points out that you are attached to your *persona*, the image you portray in the outer situation, and not giving enough attention to the inner process of individuation. Dreams sometimes offer specific messages, particularly if you are dangerously polarized and attached to an inflexible point of view. In such dreams, you may play a role that you do not like or that surprises you. Author Anne Rivers Siddons writes that "Dreams give . . . insight into what I need to work on . . . areas of pain and conflict . . . areas of focus. . . . It is important to pay attention."[7] Following is an example of a reductive compensatory dream.

I am driving down what seems to be DMH Road toward the ocean. The sun is setting. It is a beautiful warm evening. The sky is a Renoir of watercolors. I think, "I wish I had arranged to visit Joan. Perhaps I will swing by. We can have an impromptu dinner and watch the sunset." But I decide not to because I did not call in advance. The road suddenly becomes very steep with many hairpin curves. The colors are gone and the sky is dark. I can barely see. My headlights don't work. My car is going faster and faster down the hill. I am trying to keep it in control, but I can tell I am about to lose control of the car. The light is dimming. The turns come more quickly now. The car is small and low to the road. I can barely see the way ahead. I am still making the turns, but I am quickly losing control. I can't see at all now. I am trying to make my way through the dark. My headlights are out. It is as if my eyes are closed or I have gone blind. I concentrate on the feel of the road. I make several turns that way. Then I feel the car go slightly over the left edge of the road as I am taking a right curve. I feel the car begin to slide up and tip as though it is going to turn over. The left side of the car is lifting off the ground.

Then I am knocking on the front door of a house. A man and a young boy about twelve years old come to the door. The man takes me inside and down some steps and out onto a patio. He has friends over for a barbeque. I apologize for disturbing him. He says it's okay. His house is in a place where the road is particularly dangerous and this has happened before. He says he has called for help and to make myself comfortable. Help myself to food and whatever I need. He walks away.

I feel a little dazed. I don't know anyone here. I check myself to see if I am injured. I don't find anything physical, but I feel strange. I must be in shock. I stand watching the people for a while. They are all friends, chatting and laughing and enjoying being together. I talk with someone who asks if I am okay. I say I think so, but it was a really weird experience. I ask, "Have you ever had the feeling that you are driving too fast down a road with hairpin switchback curves and then you are blind? That feeling right then when I couldn't see and I switched to feeling the sensations and trying to drive by sensation alone was both frightening and exhilarating."

Then I go outside. It is daylight. I want to look at my car. I see a car. Is it mine? The car is a fancy metal soapbox style. It is a one-seater convertible. It is long and kind of boxy, but with curved edges. The blue paint on part of it has been stripped off and I can see the metal, as if it is in the process of being repainted. The engine cover is open and the engine is gone. I appear to be in a mechanical repair shop in the driveway outside the house. A couple of men are standing at a workbench. There are three or four car engines on the bench. The young boy who was at the door when I arrived is telling a man who is there to investigate my accident that the car he and I are looking at is not the same one I arrived in. He says mine was new. The man looks at the car and makes some notes. Then he asks the head mechanic which of the engines belongs to the car. The mechanic shrugs and points to the one he is working on. The investigator looks at the engine. The boy says no, that isn't it and the car body is not the same car body. The man walks along the bench looking at the engines. He is walking from left to right. As he walks, the engines are newer and in better condition. He points to the last one and says he thinks that is the one that was in my car. How can we find out? The man says he can hook it up to the monitor (which looks like a TV) and then we can see inside. The investigator says "Let's do that." I have a feeling that this shop sees a lot of accidents and they take parts from the cars and recycle them. The young boy seems to be saying that my car was in good shape when I arrived and did not need to be salvaged. I am beginning to feel more alert and ready to work with the investigator to find out what is going on.

What associations do I find in this dream? The car is a symbol of how I am making my way right now. A bit out of control, I'd say! That fits. I've been obsessing about commitment again. I have been feeling caught in that old abandonment complex. Trying to control a future over which I have very little control. I even went so far as to consider ending the relationship if we couldn't find a way to define our future. I go round and round with this one. Well, at least I survive in the dream. In fact, I do more than survive—I look inside and I change. Perhaps I'm ready to let go of my ego attachment to a specific form and try my hand with trusting what I feel.

PROSPECTIVE DREAMS

Prospective or anticipatory dreams, according to Jung, hint at what needs to be accomplished now and in the future. They may anticipate a possible negative or positive consequence of continuing a certain course of action by dramatizing the outcome in a dream story. They may portray a course of action in an emotionally exaggerated way that may puzzle or confuse you. Their purpose is to motivate you to explore other alternatives.

The difference between a prospective and a compensatory dream is that the latter presents views that have been repressed or not attended to that can increase your insight about the outer situation. Prospective dreams, on the other hand, are "an anticipation in the unconscious of future conscious achievements, something like a preliminary exercise or sketch, or a plan roughed out in advance."[8] Stephen King claims that such dreams "are a way that people's minds illustrate the nature of their problems . . . [and] illustrate the answers . . . in symbolic language."[9]

TRANSPERSONAL DREAMS

Transpersonal dreams are not exclusively about personal life experiences. They tend to be extra-numinous, and often have an ethereal or surreal quality. They pulsate with even more mystery than extrasensory and mythical dreams from the collective unconscious. While they impact your personal life, they also take you beyond your personal concerns. They have a unique enigmatic quality that often feels philosophical, metaphysical, and transcendental. I'm intuitively drawn by a mystery that arouses my curiosity. The mysterious quality present in the immediate experience of these dreams is a signal that the dream carries valuable insights that will inform me. Sometimes I find it difficult to express these dreams in a direct and linear manner. Such dreams often inspire me to write poetry.

Transpersonal dreams have the mythic energy of archetypal characters that offer wise counsel through declarations, conduct, qualities, inclinations, and convictions that strike me as coming from the voice of a master. The character may be a wise elder, the spirit of a deceased person, or a positive male or female figure. In contrast to the Wise Counselor, however, the spirit archetype may be negative and signify evil. As Jung points out we are not always able to know when evil may be necessary to produce good.[10]

Your transpersonal unconscious influences your personal and collective unconscious, and blends your personal and collective life themes with your transpersonal experiences. These dreams are palpably beyond ordinary experience; they contain the spirits, and daemons, and gods that Jung describes.[11] They may bring flashes of insight that are so profound they change you forever. Sometimes, they are extrasensory-perception (ESP) dreams that are telepathic or precognitive and foreshadow events in your life.

TELEPATHIC AND PRECOGNITIVE DREAMS

Telepathic dreams symbolically reflect an event happening at a distance from you, or foretell an event in the future. A telepathic dream does not tend to show exact images of the outer event it is reflecting or foretelling. It portrays it in a symbolic, metaphorical drama. Precognitive dreams foretell a future event in some precise and factual detail. "The more the unforeseen details of an event pile up," Jung observes, "the more definite is the impression of an existing foreknowledge."[12] The events that piled up after the series of telepathic and precognitive dreams related on pages 28–29 felt as surrealistic as the foreshadowing dreams.

A series of dreams reveals a tapestry of the unconscious motifs and archetypes that influence your emotions, your choices, your behavior, and therefore your entire life. That tapestry becomes apparent when you look back at the pattern that has unfolded across time. As you explore a series of dreams, you discover their dramatic structure in images, symbols, and metaphors that help you recognize how they are like chapters in a book about your life. My entire experience of the inner dreams and the outer occurrences in this series had an eerie synchronistic quality. The experiences hit me in such quick succession that I felt as though they came right out of the blue.

Of course, we usually only know a dream is extrasensory after the foreshadowed event has occurred. However, when you keep an ongoing record of your dreams, you begin to recognize their tone. That tone can sometimes help you recognize a precognitive or telepathic dream. You may find that your dreaming soul helps you recognize and be sensitive to specific types of future events. This specificity is related to the nature of your psyche.

A series of precognitive dreams may present a variety of themes. The common thread between them is the intensity of the future event and the impact of the event on your life. With practice, you can become more sensitive to the tone and mood of a precognitive dream. As you become more familiar with the feeling and sensation of such dreams, you are forewarned emotionally and your conscious mind is alerted to prepare for some significant change.

I had a series of three telepathic dreams that foreshadowed and reflected a tragic event in my life. The first one occurred six days before the event.

I see an image of Judy Collins (the folk singer) in which she is obviously a healer. She is sitting on the ground holding a child in her arms and singing to him. The child is dead.

I had no personal associations to the dream at the time I wrote it down. Some time after I had this dream, and after the event I will tell you about later, a client told me she saw an interview with Judy Collins in which she talked about her life being devastated by the death of her son, how she had been stretched to the limit and how, now (many years later), she is just beginning to reconnect with her music and her song writing.

Five days before the actual foretold event, I experienced a second dream as an extremely vivid and intense visual image and numinous sensory experience. There was no apparent story line, no recognizable setting, and there were no characters. There were only visual and kinesthetic sensations.

I see a visual image similar to, but not exactly like, an explosion. An eruption comes toward me, like fireworks, with very defined points and lines of sharp yellow and brilliant orange light. From a distance, it looks like an attacking entity is coming toward me—like an enormous insect with extraordinary power. I can feel the heat as the edges of the vision begin to touch my body. I wake up abruptly.

Dream images like this express forces from the collective transpersonal unconscious that, after the fact, turn out to be a precognitive foreshadowing.

The following dream, which I have titled Storm Troopers, was the final telepathic dream of the series. It was also precognitive. I had the dream on Friday the 13th, 1996, the morning Hurricane Faust struck Cabo San Lucas in Mexico, at the tip of the Baja California peninsula.

I materialize, as in Star Trek, standing in the lobby of a resort hotel. Suddenly, thunder, lightening, and rain explode out of the sky. I go outside and see many helicopters swarming overhead like storm clouds in a hurricane. Many storm troopers in camouflage uniforms and with machine guns climb down on ropes to the land. They shoot and kill people. A young boy and his father are shot as they try to get out of the pool. They fall back into the pool, their blood staining the water. I start to run, but I am told that people who try to get away are being shot.

I become invisible, rise above the chaos, and move through space. From above, I see storm troopers shooting people as they run, trying to escape into the surrounding jungle or hide under bushes. But they are routed out, and shot or stabbed with a bayonet. I do not realize that I am invisible, so I feel in danger of being shot. The ground is littered with bodies. Then I realize that the soldiers cannot see me as I pass above them.

I float above and behind a thick row of people running down a dirt path. Many of them are being shot by the soldiers on either side of the row. One man is walking against the stream of people. I recognize him. He works for the resort and now for the storm troopers. He stops one from shooting a woman he knows who is walking beneath me. I float down to the ground into the line behind her. I become visible. I move with the people into an auditorium that holds several thousand people. Storm troopers line the walls around the auditorium. The seats are full of people whispering and murmuring. I am boldly annoyed as I ask a woman behind me what is going on. She looks directly into my eyes and says, "We are demonstrating our willingness to accept this change and cooperate." A storm trooper comes out on stage. He gives an impassioned lecture. This change is necessary. We are all under his control. If we cooperate, we will be okay and, if not, we will be killed.

Then people are streaming out of the auditorium. I am directed to one area as large as a city block, where dead babies and children are lying in rows. Other blocks with rows of bodies go on as far as I can see. A storm trooper hands me a photo album (a picture book) and tells me to stand at the corner of one of the blocks. The book is open to close-up pictures of the children. Parents and family members are walking toward me. I look at the pictures. One boy with dark eyebrows and hazel eyes has a grin on his face. He has on a red knit ski cap and holds a red, white, and black Mickey Mouse doll. I glance over at the children lying in rows and I see the boy's body. A person asks me what to do. I point to the pictures, "Look at each of these pictures; if you see your child, let me know and I will show you where to claim the body." The person looks at the photographs.

At this point in the dream, my phone rang and woke me. I was crying. My chest was tight and heavy. A sharp pain stabbed my solar plexus. I was extremely sad, frightened, and anxious. The significance of this dream had to do with a current situation of which I had been unaware. The phone call was from my dear friend Linny Sanford, telling me that Hurricane Faust was battering Cabo. Later that morning, I was writing an E-mail to another close friend, Lizbeth Hamlin. I was telling her about my dream and my concern for my daughter and my future son-in-law, Eric, who were living in Cabo San Lucas, when the phone rang again. My daughter, Tej, asked in a faraway voice, "Mom, are you sitting down?" Filled with foreboding, I replied, "Yes." She recited in a flat dull voice, "Eric is dead. He has been electrocuted."

Anguish, shock, and pain exploded through me as though I had been shot in my chest by an intense blast of energy. In retrospect, I recognized that was the sensation I had had in the dream, and I also realized, based on the time difference, that Eric was being electrocuted while I was having that dream. That was its telepathic aspect.

Then I realized I would have to contact Eric's parents. That was the dream's precognitive aspect. They lived out of town; I did not know them; it took several hours to contact them. When I finally reached them, my voice was as flat and dull as my daughter's had been as I told them Eric had been killed in Hurricane Faust. They pleaded with me. "Are you certain? Could there be a mistake? Are you sure it is him?" "Yes, I am sorry to say, I'm certain," I replied, as the memory and image from the dream of me showing parents where to find the bodies of their dead children came vividly to mind.

These dreams were clearly extrasensory-perception dreams. The first two were precognitive, foreshadowing the loss that was flashing its way toward me. The first was about the death of a son. The second was of an inner explosion, like being electrocuted. The last was telepathic and precognitive. It informed me of Eric's death and foreshadowed that I would be telling his parents about their son's death.

Another aspect of ESP dreams surfaces when one person has a dream that is related to the dream of another person with whom they are emotionally close—and they have these dreams at the same time. This type of shared dream also happens between couples that regularly sleep together in the same bed. The dreams may have similar precognitions and telepathic elements, or they may contain similar images, characters, or story lines. Spaulding Gray gives an example of a precognitive dream in which he and his partner had an "overlap" of content. "I think [what] is happening often in sleep is that stuff is in the air. Like radio waves . . . they intermingle. I had a very strange experience with that and I'm not an intuitive ESP type of person."[13]

When a dream corresponds with events that happen in the outer world, it is indeed a meaningful coincidence and it catches your attention. What you might otherwise ignore or forget jerks you into emotional alertness. Your body and emotions are stirred into an intense reaction. Your mind becomes alert. You know this dream experience is important. The eerie, numinous quality of such a dream foreshadows something important, warning you to pay attention.

When you have an ESP dream, whatever quality it has, it will have a powerful effect on you. What may seem a mere coincidence to others will be undeniably meaningful to you. Although ESP dreams are less frequent than traumatic, compensatory, and prospective dreams, they have such a profound effect that they heighten your intuitive awareness and challenge you to recognize such dream experiences as links to the validity of transpersonal reality.

THE DRAMATIC STRUCTURE OF DREAMS

The stories of dreams often have a setting, a cast of characters, and a story line with discernable emotional components. These elements make up the dramatic structure of the dream. My dream stories often have elements that are familiar to me. The first thing I do with a dream is reflect on the different aspects in it to see how they represent or are symbolic of some element in my own personality. I ask myself: How am I like this or that character? How does the story line or setting in the dream reflect a situation in my outer life?

Dream Characters

The characters in your dreams may or may not be people you know. When you are currently in an active relationship with a person who appears as a character in your dream, the dream very likely reflects your involvement with that person. But it also reflects some aspect of that person as a mirror of some element of your own personality. The dream is asking you to reflect how this element may be active in your life at the time of the dream. If the character is emotionally distant, how are you behaving in an emotionally distant way?

If the character is someone you know, but with whom you are not currently emotionally involved, the dream may be a clue suggesting that you reflect about that person in the following ways: What personality characteristic and/or emotional experience of them stands out for you when you think about them now? With whom or in what situation is that characteristic and/or emotional experience active in your life at the present time? Are you paying attention to that emotion or are you ignoring it or avoiding dealing with it? The following example illustrates how a dream can be explored for its relevance to a current situation in the dreamer's life.

I am attending an informal wedding being held in a school cafeteria. I am sitting at a long table with my lover. The groom comes out on a stage. He is my first love, my high school sweetheart. He introduces the bride-to-be and wheels her out on the stage. She is sitting on a wooden stool with wheels on it. He positions her like a mannequin and she stays in that position. He jumps down off the stage, leaving her there, and walks around greeting people. I wonder if he will recognize me; when he gets to me, he smiles and kisses my cheek. I introduce him to my friend and they shake hands. I feel excited and uncomfortable.

In this example, the dreamer, a married woman, is having an affair with a married man. She is excited by the affair, but feels somewhat guilty and uncomfortable that her lover is lying to his wife. After this dream, she remembers that she was devastated when her high school sweetheart broke up with her to date a girl who would have sex with him. She reflects on ways in which she feels being a wife is like being a mannequin who is manipulated by her husband. It is more exciting to be the other woman, like the other girl her high school boyfriend dated, because then you can enjoy sex. The dreamer gradually extricated herself from the affair. In time, she divorced and was able to integrate her sexuality within a caring relationship.

Dream Settings

The settings in personal dreams are often familiar. They provide the context for your dream. For example, suppose a dream takes place in a house. The house may symbolize your psyche. The rooms in the house may represent different aspects of your psyche. The first, second, and third story, or the basement or attic, may reflect the level of the psyche and the degree of consciousness that is inspiring the dream message. Whether the house is worn down or well kept can be a reflection of the current condition of your psyche. The condition of the house and the dream's story in relation to the house may suggest something about what is going on presently in your psyche. If a dream takes place in a house where you lived in the past, the house probably represents the conditions for an emotional experience that occurred at that time. Were the earlier experiences you had in that house frightening or nurturing? The dream may be calling your attention to that house to help you think about what is similarly frightening or nurturing to you in the present. If the house is the one in which you currently live, it may represent the present concerns of your psyche. If the house is unfamiliar, it may represent that you are in the process of some new development.

The following dream is an example of how an image, in this case a house, can reflect the emotional condition of the dreamer's psyche.

I am on the ground floor of a house with a wooden floor. I can see wooden stairs in the corner that go up to the second story. I look closely at the floor. It is rotten all the way around the edges and is obviously in danger of collapsing. The wooden stairs are in need of repair and look as if they are also in danger of collapsing. I know I will have to make the repairs. It is a big job and I don't know where my tools are.

The dreamer in this example had been disabled by a deep depression for over a year. He was unable to work and was quite limited in his interpersonal relationships. He had just started dream writing and this was his first dream. He said he intuitively thought the dream felt "like the condition of my psyche. The foundation is rotten and I will have to do a lot of work to repair it." He committed to ongoing depth analysis and his dreams gradually began to reflect the repairs he was making within his psyche.

Dream Plots

The plot in personal dreams tends to be about emotional experiences. The emotions are present in story lines that involve survival, relationships, success, or failure. Each personal dream tends to focus on a situation that highlights either a specific emotion or a combination of emotions. The emotion may be fear, anger, sadness, or joy, or it may be any combination or variation of these four core emotions. Some of the themes are familiar, and some of them are unfamiliar, but, as in the following dream, they all suggest possibilities for personal growth.

I have just finished a telephone conversation with a new, but somehow familiar, friend who is a famous and wealthy man who has invited me to visit him on his estate. I walk toward his estate along a highway. The side of the road is under major construction and I am afraid and wonder if I will be able to take the turn off to the estate. When I get there, instead of a road, there is a set of steps leading up to the top of a mountain. As I climb the steps, I notice that they are being completed just ahead of me. I get to the top and on the other side I see the estate. It spreads out to the edge of the mountain and overlooks the ocean. I walk down and into the mansion looking for my friend. I see a famous movie star and many people bustling around setting up for a party. I feel sad, as if I don't belong. I don't see my friend, so I go outside and climb up further to sit in a hammock in a gazebo. I can watch from there. I see my friend sitting in a hammock below me. He looks up and waves and then climbs up to the gazebo. I feel happy as we visit and have a comfortable, funny, affectionate time.

Then we are running through a tunnel and being pursued by a high school marching band dressed as soldiers. I'm angry because a soldier tries to capture us, but my friend karate chops him and we escape through a door in the side of the tunnel. We come out of the tunnel in the city park of the town where I went to high school. The park has a gazebo, but it is dilapidated. I know my friend will fix it. I am happy to be back in this small seaside resort town. My friend and I will live there quietly. He does not want to be recognized and treated like a celebrity.

This was the dream of a woman in mid-life. She had experienced major changes and loss in all areas of her life, including the death of loved ones, financial ruin, discontent with her career, and marital separation. At first, she associated the dream to the losses she had experienced and her realization that she wanted to make major changes in her life.

Almost one year later, she remembered the dream and realized it foreshadowed those changes in ways she could not have anticipated. She had reconnected with a friend from the past in a way that was a catalyst for integrating her losses and facilitating her physical, emotional, mental, and spiritual development.

This is an example of how dreams remain vital and encourage the process of discovering new possibilities for personal, spiritual, and creative growth. The message of the dream helped her make a choice not to get enmeshed in relationships and situations based on power and control.

Dream Messages

Informed intuition is a key factor in understanding the messages in your dreams. Sometimes I gather background material to supplement my intuition. I consider myths and folklore, and the themes of novels, movies, and poetry as ways of recognizing archetypal themes in my dreams. This, along with a good working map of the psyche, increases the accuracy and depth of my dream exploration. It has taken time for me to recognize the distinctive language of my personal dreams. All dreamers have private metaphorical and mythic realities that contribute to the dramatic structure of their dreams. Therefore, the way I interpret an image may be meaningful to me, but could be meaningless to you.

If the messages of a dream seem quite obvious, I take that as a sign to probe deeper. I turn the dream around and explore what is not obvious. Jung says most dreams compensate for a one-sided conscious position that leaves out a consideration of the opposite possibility. Therefore, I try to consider what the opposite message of a particular dream would be. If a dream suggests I have been wronged, I ask how I might have wronged someone. What is the wisdom concealed behind the mask of the obvious? Often it takes a series of dreams to see what is behind the mask.

Dream writing helps you discover and honor the messages of your dreams. What does your dreaming soul want you to know? Sometimes the writing process leads to a clear interpretation of a dream that can be literally applied to your life. But even when it does not, the psychic energy generated by the writing process always broadens your conscious outlook, stimulates your curiosity, and contributes to your healing and creativity. When you do not clearly understand the message from a dream, the process of writing it, of giving it form, stirs you in a way that is a catalyst for change and, therefore, growth. When you consciously understand the symbols and metaphors of your dreams, the effect on your personal development is even more powerful.

SYMBOLS AND METAPHORS

At the symbolic level of engagement, your dreams are metaphors and experiences intended to enlighten and energize you. When you ponder your dreams and wonder what they represent and reference, in addition to their connection to your personal life, you discover a deeper intentional purpose. That purpose is to facilitate transformation in your life. This is the path of self-actualization and individuation. You get to participate in your own evolution by accepting the challenge to understand the symbolism of your dreams and, at the same time, trust and honor the directly felt sense of how the dream is relevant to your life. Dreams are intentional metaphoric images, and emotional and sensory experiences that communicate messages. When you apply the meaning of those metaphors and symbols to daily life, that application is a catalyst for transformation.

Jung speaks of metaphors in relation to the unconscious expression of archetypal content:

An archetypal content expresses itself, first and foremost, in metaphors. If such a content should speak of the sun and identify with it the lion, the king, the hoard of gold guarded by the dragon, or the power that makes for the life and health of a man, it is neither the one thing nor the other, but the unknown third thing that finds more or less adequate expression in all these similes, yet—to the perpetual vexation of the intellect— remains unknown and not fitted into a formula.[14]

When you approach a dream as a symbolic metaphor, you are challenged by that "perpetual vexation of the intellect." Your logical mind wants to understand the dream clearly and easily. But your dreams are meant to challenge you to discover what is not immediately perceptible. They require your attention in a way that exercises your intuition and your intellect. They exercise your skill with sorting out the intimate inexplicable message that the metaphor is communicating.

As you become more familiar with the metaphorical context of your dreams, you look forward to looking into the images that come through that inner door from what is beyond your conscious ego. As you live with them and write them, you begin to sense their meanings and solve their mysteries. They open to you and reveal themselves in response to the attention you turn toward them. When you make the effort to build a relationship with the metaphors presented by your dreams, you discover possibilities that are not yet known to you and create the probability of bringing about those possibilities in your life.

As I put words around the metaphors and symbols of dream experiences, it helps me to remember that a dream is an indirect reference to a pattern in my psychic life. Jung suggests that the indirect nature of dreams is intended to cause you to stretch to understand the metaphor from a deeper emotional level. "As soon as you take the . . . metaphors as symbols for something unknown, your conception of the nature of dreams at once deepens."[15]

A dream is a metaphor in which the images, characters, and themes are used to designate something else, thus making an implicit comparison. In the previous dreams, the marriage of a high school sweetheart is a metaphor for a current unrequited love. A rotten floor is a metaphor for the depressed state of the dreamer's psyche. A successful and familiar man is a metaphor for the dreamer's need to make significant changes in her life. Dreams use symbolism to show you what your dreaming soul wants you to know. They reveal, rather than conceal, something important to your individuation and growth.

Dreams provide metaphorical images and experiences that encourage wholeness. The purpose of the dream is to increase your conscious awareness in order to release your potential and broaden your experience. Dreams compensate for your conscious position by proposing a way to develop new thoughts, feelings, and behaviors in relation to your experiences. They provide what Jung calls "a possible line of advance [that you] would never have thought of."[16]

INNER WISDOM AND CREATIVITY

Through regular dream-writing practice, you can become familiar with the way your dreaming soul uses various types of dreams to motivate you toward a solution or a healthier, more creative way of living. As you deepen your understanding of your unique dream metaphors, you discover ways to create your future by fleshing out the naturally creative impulse that pours into your awareness from the world of dreams.

Many people seek answers through oracles, tarot cards, or astrology. They search for answers from other wise people or sources outside of themselves. We all learn through mentors and by apprenticeship to others. But in the end, it is important for you to develop your own inner wisdom. When you feel confident that you can consult with and trust the oracle of your inner wisdom, that source becomes even more available to you through the different types of dreams. You find the truth, wisdom, and creativity that dwells deep in your own psyche. You can deepen your search for the soulful source of your inner wisdom by focusing on remembering, meditating, and writing your dreams.

3

remembering, meditating, and writing dreams

For the layman who has done his utmost in the personal and rational
sphere of life and yet has found no meaning and no satisfaction there, it is enormously
important to be able to enter the sphere of irrational experience. The least of things with a
meaning is always worth more than the greatest of things without it.

—C. G. JUNG, *CW* 16, ¶ 96

Some people are naturally intrigued by their dreams. They remember them and want to turn their attention inward to consult and study them. Others become motivated by an outer, usually troublesome, situation in life that demands introspection. The need to understand themselves provokes them to make the effort to develop the skills to consult their dreams.

Whether or not you usually remember and record your dreams, you may find that you forget them when you first begin your dreamwriting practice. It's one of those paradoxes. You have to want to remember a dream, but, at the same time, you cannot be so attached to wanting to remember that you become frustrated when you do not. Frustration blocks your ability to remember.

When I first began what turned out to be a prototype for this dream-writing practice, I immediately stopped remembering dreams for a while. My mentor told me this occurred because I needed to be sure that my intention was to receive the dream rather than control the unconscious in order to use it as a resource. I have found that advice to be accurate in my work with clients. In my experience, the dreams that are initially the most valuable are those that are not influenced by conscious desires. When my clients have trouble remembering their dreams, I advise them to write something—anything—in their dream journal. Even just the date and some comment like "no dream memory right now" is sufficient. This devoted attention to the process seems to help reinforce your intention to remember and write dreams. Your dreaming soul begins to trust that intention and your dreams begin to flow.

Sometimes people forget their dreams because they want to avoid their message. More often, however, forgetting a dream has nothing to do with repression. You forget dreams because your brain is in a different biochemical state when you are dreaming than when you are awake. Once the biochemical state changes, if the dream has not been "downloaded" into your conscious memory, it is no longer as available to you. In other words, as you wake up, the biochemistry of your brain changes and you remember fewer details of your dreams. You have to catch the dream while your brain's chemistry is still in the dreaming condition and your dreaming soul is still absorbed in imagining the dream into being. Sometimes a dream has been downloaded, but you don't know it until something during the day triggers an image or a memory of it. I usually take that as a sign that the dream is important and make sure I write it down, even if it's on the back of a grocery receipt.

THE ART OF DREAMING

Native Americans use the symbol of a mandala for dream catching. Dream catchers are symbolic circles worn around the neck or hung near the body of a person who wants to have a dream. Made out of a natural material, they usually contain a woven web of threads that is believed to gently ensnare dream energy so that the dreamer can become aware of the dream.

In *The Art of Dreaming*, don Juan Matus, a Native American Yaqui shaman, teaches Carlos Castaneda to engage his dreaming attention so that he becomes aware that he is dreaming at the time he is dreaming. He teaches Carlos to set up his dreams by approaching them consciously and with the intention of being aware and present in them.

He advises him that he must intend to be aware that he is falling asleep by noticing the pleasant sensations of heaviness and darkness. He must learn to be aware that he is dreaming. Don Juan suggests that he do this by looking for his hands in his dreams. One way to become aware of dreams while dreaming is, while falling asleep, to think about, image, and focus on some detail with which you are completely and comfortably familiar in waking life. Focus on this detail at the same time you remain gently aware of falling asleep. As you fall toward sleep, hold the intention of seeing that detail—for instance, your hands—in a dream.

With practice, you learn to become aware that you are dreaming without disturbing the experience. In this way, you learn to engage your dreaming attention while producing a dream to create a bridge between your inner and outer reality. Don Juan refers to everyday, goals-oriented, reality as the "first attention," and the perception of the dreaming process, unusual dreamlike events and altered states of consciousness as the "second attention."

As you continue a regular dream-writing practice over time, you become increasingly aware that you are dreaming while you are dreaming. Every dream that you choose to remember and intentionally process renews and strengthens your ability to have direct experiences of your dreams. Your dreams become a constant natural part of your life and you develop your second attention, your ability to shift your focus of awareness from outer to inner experiences.

As you become more conscious of your ability to shift into second-attention awareness, you may become more aware of lucid dreams in which you feel as though you are awake inside your dreams, observing and participating in the unfolding drama. You may become aware of the many different worlds of dreams and remember vivid details of the stories, characters, and settings that combine the familiar events of the realm of the first attention with the unfamiliar events that come to you through the realm of the second attention.

Think of your dreams as dynamic objects afloat in the sea of your psyche. Left unattended, the dark dream shells that have made it to the surface fall back into the unconscious sea of sleep. As they sink out of sight, they drift down slowly, gliding through the thick, rich stuff that makes up the elixir of your psyche and your soul. Some dream shells drop to the bottom quickly, suddenly, abruptly, leaving behind them a tight whirlpool path that spirals up to the surface and brings forth an indistinct image or a vague emotional sense of excitement or confusion.

Other dreams bump against each other and other creatures in the sea as they fall. The contact changes them. As they bump, they stir the elixir; a pocket of churning energy buoys each shell for a moment, or bounces it away into a new trajectory from which it gradually sinks back into its descent. The dreams that sink all the way to the bottom often disappear from your memory completely. They lie underneath your awareness, on the vast ocean-like floor of your psyche, waiting to rise again another night when certain currents begin to stir in a vaguely familiar pattern.

Some dreams come to rest part way down or just beneath the surface of your awareness, however. Like succulent oysters, they enclose the most delicious morsels of mystery. Juicy bits of your inner world are held securely inside each tightly clenched shell.

Like a scuba diver, you want to observe the life beneath your psychic sea, to experience the parts of yourself that dwell in that sea. Breathing meditation can act as a life-support system in this process. It breathes for you and buoys you so you can hang quietly in the depths and study the movement of the shells that contain your dreams and become familiar with their habits and their habitat. Take mental notes as you quietly and gently observe them from a distance, as if you had telescopic vision. Focus your keen inner vision and realize that you are observing your own inner life from a distance. Watch the images and dramas taking place within your dreams. Watch, wait, and remember. In this depth, you can experience the source of your being and your inspiration.

When your heart is still and your mind quiet and patient, you can observe your dreams like this—like a scuba diver, in a nonordinary state in which what you experience connects you with your inner life and creative imagination. Once you come to the surface and wake up, your luminous dreaming experience fades and gradually disappears. But you can remember much of what you experienced with your inner eye. This memory keeps you in a respectful relationship with the part of yourself that remains behind in the depths, in your dreaming soul. When you are patient, you can remember what you saw in your own depths and bring the current and the rhythm of your dreams into your life.

I am not always patient. Sometimes I forget to wait and allow the rhythm of a dream to unfold. My desire to capture the dream is like plunging a greedy hand into my internal sea. The more I try to grasp

the shell of a dream, the faster it scurries away. I pursue it and sometimes I wrap my grasping fingers around it. "Gotcha!" I chortle tri-
umphantly, as I wedge my thumbnail in between the softened edges of
its dark shell. I have abandoned my commitment to keep a respectful
distance from my dreaming soul. My aware ego is intent upon prying
open the dream shell and scooping out its elusive treasure. When I
succeed and pry the shell open, it is often empty, or what I find is not
succulent or satisfying. And sometimes, despite my grasping, or perhaps because of it, the shell wriggles free and sinks out of sight. I'm
disappointed; I thought I had snared a good one only to discover,
when I open my eyes, that the shell containing the dream has flopped
back into the elixir, leaving me with only the remnants of a vague
memory.

When you treat your dreams with gentle, respectful attention, they
tend to stay with you; they open to you and contribute to your growth.
Sometimes you may even feel your dream seeking you! It is awesome
when one of those dream shells rises out of the inner sea of your psyche and willingly falls open to your awareness, revealing something of
great value. Such dreams are lucid, clear, here-and-now experiences.

FOCUS AND MEDITATION

Dr. Jonathan Young, who organized the Joseph Campbell Library at
Pacifica Graduate Institute, told me that Campbell, who was the
author of many books on mythology, was once asked if he meditated
or had a regular form of spiritual practice. He answered, "Yes, I
underline sentences."

Anything you do with focused, centered intention and concentration can be thought of as a form of meditation. Remembering, recording, writing, and contemplating your dreams is a form of meditation.
I focus on my breath as the physical path to this meditative state.

Physical Sensations of Breath Meditation

If you already meditate or have other methods to center and focus your awareness, you can adapt those skills for dream-writing practice. If not, try the meditation method described in Exercise I on page 49. Practice every night as you go to sleep to prepare yourself to experience, remember, and record your dreams.

You may feel certain sensations in your body when you do centering meditation. As you breathe and release muscle tension, your body may feel heavy and even a little achy. If you stay with it, after a while you may feel as if you are floating or weightless. This is natural and indicates you are moving from an ordinary state of consciousness into a meditative state. If you find this uncomfortable, simply wiggle a finger. If you need to come out of the meditation, wiggle more fingers and stretch, take a deep breath, and open your eyes.

While you are meditating, you may experience sensations of tingling and warmth. That happens as your body lets go of tension at a very deep muscular and vascular level. Both the voluntary muscles of your outside body and the involuntary muscles of your inside body are expanding. If you feel dizzy or lightheaded, it only means you are getting too much oxygen. If that happens, stop the process as described above and breathe regularly for a few minutes, until the sensation goes away. Then begin the breathing again in a more subtle way. Experiment until you can breathe in a way that is comfortable for you and still follow the pattern that is described in Exercise I. When your breathing pattern is calm and centered, you will feel calm and centered.

You may also experience emotional sensations in your body as you meditate. That is good. Be willing to breathe into those sensations and allow yourself to experience them. Continue to breathe and imagine the breath flowing into the area of your body where you feel the sensations.

You do not need to understand what you are feeling. Simply continue to breathe into the sensations and notice what you experience. When you can allow yourself to feel those sensations and breathe into them, the energy they hold is released and the sensations should decrease. If you feel overwhelmed by emotional sensations, seek professional guidance.

Breathing and Centering

As you practice Exercise 1, you will become more comfortable and familiar with the breathing pattern that helps you center yourself. Your body and mind become soft and calm and quiet. You gradually soften your thoughts by repeatedly returning your attention to experience the pattern of your breath. When you find your mind wandering, follow the path of your breath. As you breathe in through your nose, follow the sensation in your body as your breath travels down through your chest and your abdomen expands.

When you expand your abdomen, you make room for your diaphragm muscle to relax. Visualize your diaphragm. It is a flat muscle that stretches horizontally through your body right under your ribs. It tends to tighten and move up under your ribs when you are stressed and not paying attention to your breathing. Picture your diaphragm relaxing and hanging loosely like a hammock. A relaxed diaphragm makes room in your chest for your lungs to inflate to their full—but still comfortable—capacity. Never strain any part of your body when you do breath work.

Continue to notice the sensations in your body as you follow your breath in a circular motion as it comes in through your nose and fills your lungs, then travels down as though it were filling and expanding your belly. Follow the sensation of your inhalation down into your belly, and the sensation of your exhalation back up through your chest and out through your mouth.

As your breathing becomes calm and regular and your muscles relax, your body can absorb the oxygen and nutrients it needs. Your breath delivers what is needed to every cell in your body. As your body absorbs what your breath brings, it feels satisfied and calm. Your mind will follow and become calm. When both your body and your mind are calm, you will experience the sensation of being centered.

Try practicing Exercise I every night as you go to sleep to increase your ability to center. In time, you will be able to create that feeling most of the time whenever you choose. Practice now as you read the exercise. If you practice while you read, even though your eyes are open, you may experience some degree of increased calmness. This is the beginning of feeling centered.

You may find it helpful to record the meditation and play it as a guide until you are familiar with the experience. If you record the meditation, speak slowly and pause at appropriate places to pace yourself.

Exercise 1:
Breathing and Centering Meditation

Focus your intention on relaxing and meditating to turn your attention inward. As you relax and turn your attention inward, close your eyes and scan your body. Relax every muscle, from the top of your head to the tips of your toes. Notice your breathing. Take several full breaths in through your nose. As you expand your abdomen, begin to exhale slowly and completely through your mouth. As you exhale, let go of all the tension in your body. Allow your breathing to continue to become calm and rhythmic.

As you continue to relax every muscle in your body, intend and allow your thoughts to begin to slow down. Just notice them and allow them to pass by without getting involved with them. Don't attach yourself to or concern yourself with your thoughts one way or the other. Instead, return your focus to your breathing and to relaxing your body. Focus on the sensation of your breath.

Count slowly to four as you inhale and follow your breath. As you bring your breath in through your nose and follow the sensation as it travels down into the top and then into the bottom of your lungs, imagine your breath passing down through your diaphragm and into your abdomen. Pause for a second as you reach the number four and your abdomen expands. Slowly begin to exhale to the count of six. When you reach six, finish the exhalation through your mouth.

Continue this until you can feel your body relax and your mind become quiet. Before you open your eyes and begin your writing, imagine what you want to focus on as you write. When you are ready, slowly count to five and then open your eyes.

◆ ◆ ◆

DREAM MEDITATION AND WRITING

Deep meditation for twenty minutes or longer is best done as a "time out" practice to develop skill in shifting your state of awareness into the second attention. The experience of centering while remembering or writing a dream is a different experience than practicing before sleep or for general centering and relaxation. Exercise 2 illustrates this point.

Exercise 2:
Dream Meditation

Focus your intention on relaxing and meditating to turn your attention inward. Begin dream meditation as you go to sleep. Visualize and feel yourself dropping down as your mind's eye travels inward to meet your dreaming soul. Anticipate your dreams with the interest and curiosity you would have when you are about to enjoy a play or movie. Look forward to dropping down into dream sleep. As you watch your dreams unfold in three dimensions on the private movie screen of your sleeping mind, be willing to wake up just enough to write or tape-record them. I record all of my dreams on a small, digital voice recorder because when I don't have to wake up to write them, I stay more involved in the experience of the dream. Many times, when I transcribe them, I find I have no memory of having recorded some of my dreams. As I transcribe them, sometimes I remember them and sometimes I don't. Either way, I feel pleased that I have a dream that otherwise may have been lost. Many of my clients prefer to voice-record their dreams and transcribe them later for these same reasons.

When you transcribe your dreams in written form, either directly from your experience of a dream or from a tape recording, drop back into the experiential memory as deeply as possible so you can feel the dream coming to life again.

Practice observing a dream while it continues. This will help keep your conscious ego from interfering with the natural unfolding of the dream. The first purpose of this dream-writing practice is for personal and creative development. So for now, let your dreams speak to you. Don't intentionally try to influence or change them. Concentrate on becoming aware that you are dreaming while you are experiencing the dream and pay attention to what happens as you observe a spontaneous dream. These dreams are certain not to be contrived and therefore give you valuable guidance in your personal and transpersonal growth.

As you record your dream, write it as if you are experiencing it at the time you are writing. Enter a meditative state by shifting your intention and your attention away from the outer realm of what is going on around you by remembering, concentrating on, and re-experiencing some aspect of the dream. This helps you return to the inner realm where the dream originated and remember the content.

As you re-engage the dream, gently intend to track the memory at the same time you are recording or writing what you notice. You will learn to shift back and forth between the dream and writing the dream. At first, you are primarily a receptive recorder, a kind of scribe, for the original dream. You want to write the dream as it came out of your passive imagination. Do not encourage the dream to continue to unfold until later, when you decide to do a visionary meditation (which I will discuss in chapter 6).

◆ ◆ ◆

In this form of meditation, you choose how deep you want to go depending on the purpose of the meditation. Before writing, go only as deep as is necessary to be able to focus and concentrate on the experience of the dream without being diverted by intruding thoughts or outside distractions. Begin by relaxing your body and regulating your breathing for a few seconds or a few minutes. Then write the original dream in the first-person fast-narrative form described on pages 58–61.

Once you feel centered, shift your mental attention toward the memory of the dream. Pay less attention to following your breath and focus on remembering, sensing, and visualizing the dream as you drop back into the experience. The process of following the memory of the dream takes the place of a mantra or some other point of concentration. You will learn to return to your breathing and centering as you continue to remember and write. With practice, your ability to center and write in a calm, alert state will become almost automatic.

Try noticing when you are in that reverie between sleeping and waking where you become aware of a dream. Notice the dream, breathe and center, and gently focus your awareness on the dream, instead of moving along into the waking state. Visualize and follow the dream as it unfolds, and replay it in your mind's eye before you open your eyes. If you wake up too quickly and begin thinking either too intensely about a dream or about the coming day, the dream will tend to vanish.

Replay what you remember with your eyes closed as often and as long as necessary to stay in touch with the dream. This is the way to transfer it into your conscious memory. When you are ready to begin dream recording or writing, take several breaths to center again in order to remember and record the dream. Try not to direct and control your images or thoughts and feelings about the dream. Just notice what happens.

As you continue, over time, to remember and record dreams, your ability to contact the source of your creative imagination grows stronger. As you repeatedly focus on the memory of a dream while you breathe, center, and hold the balance between the dream state and the waking state, you develop the ability to do the same thing with your more intentional writing.

Dreams are treasure maps showing the way to healing and creative development. They are waiting for you to discover them beneath the surface of everyday awareness. Personal dreams are about the past, the present, or some future potential. Those that are not specifically personal emerge from the deeper collective and transpersonal passive imagination. You will recognize the source and the message of dreams as you develop more reliable contact with unconscious resources. In time, you will be able to request a dream that will assist you.

REQUESTING A DREAM

To request a dream about a specific issue, reflect on what you would like your dreaming soul to consider. Hold a focus statement in your awareness as you fall asleep. Focus on your emotional experience, as well as the images and words you use to describe it. As you drift asleep, drowsily notice and feel the changes in your body and sense your inner awareness as you seek contact with your dreaming soul. As you become familiar with the felt experience of connecting yourself to your dreaming soul, it becomes a natural and recognizable experience. Exercise 3 can help you meet your dreaming soul and request a dream. As you read this exercise, picture yourself practicing as you prepare to enter sleep each night. Once you are familiar with it, vary it to meet your personal needs. If you tape-record it, use a soft voice and speak slowly, adding frequent pauses to pace yourself.

Exercise 3:
Requesting a Dream

Focus your intention on relaxing and meditating to turn your attention inward. Close your eyes and scan your body as you slowly begin to relax every muscle, from the top of your head to the tips of your toes. Notice your breathing. Take several full breaths in through your nose as you expand your abdomen. Then exhale slowly and completely through your mouth. As you exhale, let go of all tension in your body. Allow your breathing to become calm and rhythmic as you continue to relax every muscle in your body. Allow and imagine your thoughts beginning to slow. Just notice them and allow them to pass by without getting involved in them. Return your focus to your breathing and to relaxing your body.

When you feel comfortably relaxed, imagine and sense a connection with your dreaming soul. Visualize your dreaming soul by letting a picture form in your mind's eye. The image may take a specific or a nonspecific form. Allow it to take shape through color, light, and movement. Notice how the image communicates with you through gesture or speech.

Intend and feel awareness flowing between you and your dreaming soul. Ask your dreaming soul to give you a dream and trust the dream to come to you. As you drift off to sleep, repeat your focus statement and allow yourself to disengage from the outer world. Focus your awareness on your internal experience. Notice the pleasant heaviness and darkness of falling asleep as you journey inward to the realm of your dreams. Allow your breathing to remain calm and rhythmic as you relax and let yourself sleep.

Visualize your dreaming soul, request a dream, and sleep. Record or write down each dream as you become aware of it. When possible, record or write while you are still feeling as though you are experiencing the dream. It takes practice to learn how to balance between the sensory experience of the dream state and the sensory experience of the awake state of awareness.

◆   ◆   ◆

Write or tape-record every dream or fragment of a dream you remember. Do not take a chance that you will remember a dream and write or record it later. You will forget part, if not all, of it if you wait to record it. By making a record even when a dream seems vague, unimportant, or just a flash of an image, you let your dreaming soul know that you are paying attention. When you record even the slightest impression of a dream, you continue to send the message to your dreaming soul that you are interested in what is going on in your creative unconscious. If you keep sending the message, you will receive a response. Then your dreams become increasingly available and vivid.

If you are left with a vague feeling but no images, record the feeling: "I felt sad, happy, angry, pleased, afraid, confident, passionate, lethargic." Describe any sense you have of the dream: "It was dark, light, cold, hot, hard, soft, sweet, sour, wet, dry." Jot down your impressions, even if you think they are meaningless.

When you record what you remember without censoring or without adding to it, you receive increasingly clear and distinct images, words, and themes as you remember your dreams. If you use a tape recorder, transcribe dreams into written form as soon as possible. As you write in your journal from the taped version, focus upon remembering and re-experiencing the dream. The written form of your dream is the first part of your dream-writing practice. It is important to feel the experience of the dream as much as possible as you write, so that the written version, whenever possible, is more than a distant recorded echo of the dream.

As you continue dream writing, you learn to stay, at least partially, in the biochemical dream state while you record the dream. You feel dreamy, yet aware. You are in a reverie similar to a light hypnotic trance or meditative state as you re-enter the dream and record what you see, hear, feel, taste, and touch. Don't forget to include your emotional experience.

When you learn to maintain the reverie, you imprint a memory in your conscious mind that you can refer to as you write. You can then move back and forth between the felt experience of the dream and the memory of it. As you write the first draft, you imprint the memory more clearly in your conscious mind. Then you have a file of mindful memories of dreams that is very valuable for recognizing related themes over time.

REPETITIVE DREAM THEMES

Multiple dreams in one night are often connected sequentially by some common thread—a theme, image, emotion, or symbol. Some dreams are connected from one night to the next. On the other hand, several nights, weeks, months or even years may pass before a dream with a similar or related theme appears.

Thoughtfully observe the unique and repetitive themes in your dreams. Attending to the themes helps you recognize the significance and purposefulness of a series of dreams. It also seems to encourage certain themes to repeat in your dreams when an old emotional or behavioral pattern crops us. You discover over time that you have dreams with certain repetitive elements and that they have addressed similar patterns from your past. When you recognize the theme, you can look for ways in which you may be re-enacting an old pattern in your outer life.

For example, I, like many other people, have had a repeated dream in which I am back in college. In my dream, I usually feel confusion or failure regarding an algebra assignment. I've forgotten it, or can't understand how to do it, or I'm late for class, or I can't find the class-room. Over the years, variations on this dream have occurred whenever I was grappling with some challenge that required me to take responsibility to solve a problem in my life. When this dream happens, I know I am avoiding the hard work of finding my own solution. Often, I am in denial and the dream is calling my attention to that fact. I have learned to recognize that, when I have the Algebra Dream, I need to explore what I am not tracking efficiently in my outer life.

Needless to say, I was thrilled not long ago when I had the Algebra Dream and, in the dream, I not only understood the problem I was working on, I solved it and graduated out of the class! Yahoo! However, I must add that I continue to have dreams in which I am back in some sort of educational environment. They seem to correlate with outer experiences in which I need to contemplate the situation and, perhaps, make a change.

You can learn to recognize dreams with related themes or characters by keeping a record over time. The only way you can discover the connection between your dreams is to keep and read a sequence of them. Keep in mind that the sequence may take place in one night or over many nights, weeks, months, or years. The thread of a repetitive theme that runs through dreams reveals specific aspects of which you must become conscious to support your personal development. As you pick up each thread of a theme and examine it for how it may be active in the present, you recognize the pattern in your daily life. Then you can figure out what actions you want to take to change the negative patterns, and to generate positive possibilities. Once you take effective action, your dreams begin to reflect the healing that results and support continued progress.

My dream exploration keeps me in constant touch with what I know, and what my dreaming soul knows about how my dream themes help me heal, grow, and develop my creative potential. The wisdom I receive from dreams for personal healing and creative growth always helps me clarify my personal position on an issue and reconnect with my personal identity. In the process, I discover my authentic voice and develop the ability to speak with confidence, clarity, and truth. A particular kind of creativity stirs when I attend to my dreams.

As you gain the skills to recognize past and present information from dreams and life, your conscious awareness expands, deepens, and differentiates. Perceptions, beliefs, and prejudices regarding a variety of experiences are clarified and integrated. Dream themes help you recognize the boundaries between fantasy and reality, while experiencing and respecting how flexible and transparent those boundaries often are. Devoted dream work always leads to self-discovery and personal development. The discovery is not always pleasant, but when it is integrated, it is always a movement toward creativity. As you remember and assimilate dreams, life transforms and develops in new ways.

WRITING YOUR DREAMS

I always begin by recording and then writing the first draft of a dream in the first-person, present-tense, fast-narrative style. This style describes what is happening in the dream story from your perspective as a participant. You may be a participating character, or you may be an observing character. The purpose is to tell the story as if it were happening as you write. Write as though you are participating and/or observing and describe what is happening and what you see. What do you see through the eyes of the participant? What do you see through the eyes of the observer?

To do this, reenter the memory of the dream as described on pages 51–53. This first writing is like a rough draft of a story that is developing out of your spontaneous passive imagination. As you write this rough draft, you may feel as if you are taking dictation from an inner author. Or you may feel as if you are making a word sketch of an image, feeling, sensation, or symbol.

When I write in the first person, present tense, I write fast, with the intention of describing the entire experience as completely as possible. I use fast-narrative writing to record whatever I observe or experience as I remember the dream. I write what happens as it happens, as if I were still experiencing the dream. Later, I go back and fill in details, speculations about, and associations to the dream.

The first-person, present-tense, fast-narrative writing style is often used in the first phases of writing fiction. The goal is to move the story, in this case the dream story as you remember it, through time and space, with enough detail to paint a word picture of the experience. It is like a rough draft that you will come back to later and expand. Here is an example of a dream described in the first-person, present-tense, fast-narrative style.

I am with my parents on their sailboat, which is large enough for five. We are out at sea and I am bitching, as usual, because I don't like being on the boat. I am seasick. It starts to storm and rain. I can see a small boat coming through the rain. It pulls up next to us.

There is a man on it holding a yellow balloon. Dad says he can come aboard until the storm is over. He looks like Jack Nicholson in "The Shining." Really creepy. He comes aboard and tells us we should be careful with his balloon.

There are wedding rings tied to the end of the string on the balloon. He says he doesn't want it to get away or he will lose the rings. I do something and the balloon flies up in the air. He starts screaming at me just like in "The Shining." The balloon goes up and breaks, but the string gets caught in the mast so the rings are still there.

Then the weather clears and we land in Bora Bora. It is beautiful. I get off the boat and tell my mom, "Mom, I don't like that guy. He really pissed me off yelling at me that way." I can feel the movement of the boat while I am dreaming. And then I wake up. It was so real!

My daughter had this dream some time after the death of her fiancé. It points out in symbolic form some of the core dynamics of her relationship with him and with her father and me. I want to protect her privacy, so I will not analyze these aspects. I present the dream primarily so you can notice how she uses the first-person point of view and the present tense. It is a good idea to check first dream drafts to make sure you are using "I" and the present tense: "I am, I see, I hear, I tell, I touch, I feel, I laugh." My daughter describes the sensation she feels in her body with the movement of the boat on the water. The use of descriptive words gives a feel for the emotional and sensual experiences of her dream. This language allows her to re-engage the experience of the dream through her sensual memory when she returns later to expand this first draft.

Begin to record and write your dreams in the first-person, present-tense, fast-narrative form as soon as possible. If you do not have a fresh dream, use one from the past. Practice by describing any experience in the first-person, present-tense, fast-narrative style until you are familiar and comfortable with writing that way.

Remember that the purpose of this style of writing is to allow you to stay as close as possible to the immediate experience of the dream by writing it as if it were happening as you write. This gives you experience with the skill of writing from an intentionally chosen point of view, a skill that is valuable in all forms of expressive and creative writing. Exercise 4 will help you practice first-person, present-tense, fast-narrative writing.

Exercise 4:
First-person, Present-tense,
Fast-narrative Writing

Choose a dream, focus your intention on relaxing and meditating to turn your attention inward, and return to the memory of the dream in your visual and sensory imagination. Write the dream in first-person, present-tense, fast-narrative style, based on what you see and feel as it unfolds in your memory.

When the dream is vivid, describe details as you write, if you can do so without losing sight of the ongoing story. But if you sense the story fading, return to the basic theme and keep writing until you have completed the plot of the dream story. Elaborate on details after you have written the basic story line.

◆　◆　◆

As you continue to write your dreams, you become familiar with the first-person, present-tense point of view, a key element in the craft of creative writing. Dream writing also helps you develop other specific writing skills. You can use the images, metaphors, and emotions from dream writing as springboards to dive into visionary meditation and dream-story writing. We will learn about visionary meditation writing in chapter 6. For now, any element of a dream can serve as a spring-board to drop down into visionary meditation so you can become present with what you notice and give it written form. Strong emotions are often one of the most noticeable elements of a dream.

Feeling and Writing Strong Dream Emotions

One of the main conduits to and from your dreams is the emotional experience you have in and of the dream. Use those feelings to express your experience of the dream through word pictures. Focus on anything that catches your attention and put words around it. Focus on the theme, a character, or the setting as it relates to your emotional experience of the dream.

In time, you will use some aspect of your dream material as a springboard to move from the passive imagination that created the dream to the active imagination or visionary meditation in which you write the dream forward. Visionary-meditation writing is a way you can build a bridge between the passive, receptive awareness of your inner unconscious material and your ability to consciously respond to that material. Later, you may choose to continue the material into prose or poetry. This is one way you can develop your creative writing skills.

My enthusiasm for and dedication to this form of meditative practice becomes stronger as I continue to write my dreams. The process requires commitment and focus. Each of us has a personal learning curve that determines how long it takes to master a new set of information and apply it to life. As you move along your learning curve, you go through several phases. The first is unconscious incompetence—when you don't know what you don't know. The second is conscious incompetence—when you know that you don't know much. The third is unconscious competence—when you don't know what you know. Finally, you achieve conscious competence—when you can trust what you know and use what you have learned creatively.

It is easy to continue along your learning curve in dream writing if you enjoy dreaming and writing. In return for the insight and creativity you gain, you devote yourself to doing what you love on a regular basis. When you do, you develop an ability to understand dreams that helps you gain insight into yourself and others. This is a foundation for creative and spiritual expression.

Flagging Dreams for Further Exploration

As your journal of dream writing grows, flag the dreams you want to work with so you can return to them. I flag my dreams according to the most powerful and/or repetitive symbols. For instance, I put a sticky note on each of my "algebra" dreams so I can look at the dream context of that theme over time.

Flagged dreams and the visionary meditation narratives that you write from them can be ideas and images you use later for writing prose and poetry. You increase your insight into the meaning of your dreams by looking at them as stories with a dramatic structure.

The dreaming soul that creates a dream often presents a story that follows the same dramatic structure you find in novels, poetry, and other forms of creative writing. As you study and write this form as it appears in your personal dreams, you understand more about your dreams and you strengthen your ability to use dramatic structure when you write prose and poetry.

fleshing out
personal
dream stories

*Coming now to the form of dreams, we find everything from
lightning impressions to endlessly spun out dream-narrative. Nevertheless
there are a great many "average" dreams in which a definite structure
can be perceived, not unlike that of a drama.*

—C. G. JUNG, *CW* 8, ⁋ 651

Once you have recorded a dream, explore it as a metaphor for what
it suggests about your personal life. How is the dream presenting
something relevant to your personal life now? How does it speak to a
current physical, emotional, mental, or spiritual issue in your life?

To answer these questions, you need to delve deeper than your first
intuitive sense of the meaning of the dream. In fact, the more obvious
the meaning of the dream seems to you, the more you need to explore
it to discover its deeper meaning. Trust your intuition; it is giving you
one perspective. But then dig deeper. The content of your dreams may
range from fragmented images, vague feelings, and sensations to fully
fleshed out sequences of detailed dramatic plots.

You flesh out a dream when you remember memories and outer experiences that seem related to it. Write down your first hunches about the dream. This is the time in dream-writing practice to journal your spontaneous associations. Let yourself brainstorm and write anything and everything that occurs to you about the dream. The purpose of journaling is to release, express, and process your thoughts, feelings, and associations to your dreams and your life experiences. But don't stop there. Chances are your first hunch is only one aspect of what the dream has to offer. Exercise 5 on page 69 gives you some guidance in this process.

As you flesh out your dreams, they begin to make sense. When you pay attention to their dramatic structure, you see that they contain images, feelings, and sensations that are meant to remind you of past experiences or experiences that are not yet directly accessible to your conscious awareness. These dreams have themes and characters that draw your attention to opportunities for your development. Some nontrauma-related repetitive dreams draw attention to certain attitudes, behavior patterns, or emotional reactions that are at cross purposes with your individuation. They may even suggest ways of changing those patterns.

It is important to explore your dreams for their personal meaning before you look for their creative, transpersonal, and spiritual potential. Begin by treating every dream theme as a metaphor from your personal unconscious. The first purpose of the dream is to encourage you to reflect on the current events in your life and then upon repetitive patterns of behavior and the situations in which they occur.

For instance, a dream may be about an unresolved situation in your personal life that you do not recognize or have responded to inadequately or mistakenly. When you amplify and flesh out such a dream with self-reflective personal and cultural associations, it helps you clarify and solve the unresolved issues. When you reflect upon the dream, you discover alternative affective and effective responses that help you resolve problems and increase the energy available to you for creative expression.

Personal dreams may also contain images and themes from the genetic memories of your collective unconscious. Do what you can to gather details about the historical, ethnic, and cultural background of your family of origin. Stories from your family members and other sources about the mythology and history of your ethnic and cultural background provide you with the most relevant information to help you understand the symbolic meaning of some of the themes and archetypes in your dreams.

Although family and cultural associations are important to amplify and expand the possible meaning of a dream, the most valuable associations are the ones that are meaningful to you. Pay attention to and record the most vivid feelings, images, and ideas that spontaneously come to mind when you are reviewing a dream. If no spontaneous associations occur to you, check outside resources to help you flesh out the dream material. When you explore symbolic images in a dream, use a variety of resources. Although prepared dream dictionaries may be helpful, be careful not to take them too literally. They are limited, because they reflect the associations and research of the people who wrote them, not yours, so they may not apply to you.

A dream may seem to be inspired by something you have read, or a movie, or something you have heard or seen on the news. That does not mean the dream is necessarily about that event. It means that your dreaming soul has chosen those experiences to illustrate a certain kind of issue. Some questions that are useful when reflecting upon a dream include: What do you think this dream is trying to illustrate? What emotions do you feel in this dream? Does it remind you of anything from your past? Does it remind you of anything going on in your life right now? Are you involved with any of the characters in the dream at the present time? If so, what is the nature of that involvement?

The theme of a dream always has personal relevance for you. It may be something that has not occurred to you, or something you have not resolved, or something you ignored because you just didn't want to deal with it. When my friend Kali was a little girl, she used to tell her father "I can't want to, Dad. It's too hard!" We all feel like that at times. Dream-writing practice can be hard, but it can help you resolve issues and gain access to the psychic energy necessary for your personal and creative development.

Dream motifs are generated by the physical, emotional, mental, and spiritual experiences you have that inform your passive imagination. They are influenced by the ideas and beliefs you have formed based upon those experiences. Their mythic story quality is presented as vague or vivid images that unfold over the course of the dream. The dramatic structure of your dreams mirrors the issues you are processing in your outer life as well as what is developing within your unconscious psyche. Examine details such as the point of view, setting, plot, characters, dialogue, and emotional and sensual experiences of the dream.

In the course of this dream-writing practice, you explore the use of dramatic structure and study the dynamics of a variety of dream motifs. You build your descriptive vocabulary as you put words around writing from a particular point of view. You increase your ability to develop the setting in which the drama takes place. You practice following and developing the plot, flesh out and develop the characters and dialogue, and amplify the emotional and sensual experiences of your dreams. In the process, you are likely to come to a deeper understanding of the metaphors of your dreams. You will naturally increase your creative writing skills as you practice the art of describing the stories that are your dreams. Exercise 5 can help you flesh out spontaneous associations to dreams. It is also an excellent way to develop imaginative visualization skills that can inform your creative writing.

Exercise 5:
Fleshing Out Personal Dream Associations

Focus your intention on relaxing and meditating to turn your attention inward. Ask: What in the dream grabs my attention? What has the most energy for me? What feels most important to me? Highlight or underline the characters, their actions and words, and the key elements in the setting and the theme of the dream. After you have done this, draw a line. Use what you have highlighted as a springboard for writing your personal, cultural, and archetypal associations and amplifications.

First, journal personal associations in a stream-of-consciousness, brainstorming style. When reviewing the dream, write whatever occurs to you without censoring anything. Personal associations are thoughts, memories, emotions, and sensations related to the dream. They include your connections, speculations, and possible interpretations both during and after the dream experience. Write about how the dream reflects people, events, feelings, desires, anxieties, thoughts, and conflicts in your waking life and environment. Does a dream reflect the attitudes and beliefs in your family and the environment in which you were brought up? Journal about other dreams you have had that seem related through theme, character, setting, or emotional tone, to the dream you are working with.

Practice expanding your dream material with these associations. As you read your fast narrative, use your imagination to feel your way back into the dream memory. As you revisit the dream experience, take care to leave it as undisturbed as possible. Try to be in the memory, without changing it. This allows you to come closer to the soulful quality of the dream material. Remember and visualize the dream with the intention of being in touch with the feelings and images. Notice what it is about. Is there a story line? Are there particularly vivid images, verbal dialogues, or statements? Stay close to the dream as an immediate experience.

◆ ◆ ◆

POINT OF VIEW

Your point of view in a dream is determined by the role you play in it. You are usually, but not always, the central protagonist character known as the "dream ego." Note how the first-person, present-tense, fast-narrative style can reflect this point of view:

I am standing inside a lobby of what appears to be a large resort hotel. Many people are running in a panic all around me. Suddenly, I am outside the lobby . . . then I am floating up in the air. . . . I am floating above a crowd of people. . . . I see a soldier point a gun at a woman on the ground.

With this point of view, you remain inside the experience of the dream and write from that perspective. This may feel awkward at first. It is common to switch to the observing past tense without realizing it. This will distance you from the dream in a way that causes you to lose some of your direct experience. For example, the above narrative in the observing past tense reads:

I was standing inside a lobby of what appeared to be a large resort hotel. Many people were running in a panic all around me. Suddenly, I was outside the lobby . . . then I was floating up in the air. . . . I was floating above a crowd of people. . . . I saw a soldier point a gun at a woman on the ground.

Notice which point of view you are taking at any given time. When your perspective throughout the dream is that of an observer watching the dream drama but not participating, you are, in fact, actually participating, but as the omniscient observer. As the omniscient observer, you see everything, but you do not participate or feel involved. From the observer point of view, the above example reads like this:

I observe myself, as though from a distance. I see myself standing inside a lobby of a large resort hotel. I see many people running in panic all around me. Then I see myself outside the lobby. . . . I watch myself float up in the air above a crowd of people. At the same time, I observe as one soldier points a gun at a woman on the ground.

Sometimes you, as the dreamer, move back and forth within the dream between being the observer and being the participant. When you are a participant, maintain that point of view when you write the dream in order to stay as close to the original experience as possible. When you are an observer, write from that point of view, but be careful to stay in touch with the images and emotional and sensory experiences that are seen through the eyes of the participant character. In this case, the above example reads:

I can see myself from a distance, as if I were up in a corner near the ceiling. I see myself standing inside a lobby that is large and is decorated like a beach resort. Then I am inside my body and I can see many people running in panic all around me. Then suddenly, I am outside the lobby. I am in my body floating up in the air . . . from up there I look down at a crowd of people . . . they are all running. . .

One more thing about point of view. Psychologically, the point of view that you, as the dreamer, have in the actual dream tends to reflect how conscious you are of the issues the dream presents. When you are participating in a dream, your perspective tends to reflect issues and situations of which you are at least somewhat conscious. When you, as the dreamer, are observing a dream, your perspective tends to reflect less-conscious issues or newly emerging possibilities.

DREAM STORIES

Dream stories often present a series of events in which some connection between the events is inferred and at times clearly established. When you think of a dream as a story taking place in your psyche, you can begin to recognize the elements of the narrative: setting, plot, images, characters, and events—the elements of all good storytelling. These elements may reflect a familiar personal, psychological, or mythological motif. They may be based on a collective myth such as the hero's journey, or on a personal motif such as whether to do what you want to do or what another person asks you to do. These elements all make up the context of your dreams.

SETTING

Another important element of your dream story's dramatic structure is its setting—where the dream is taking place. The dream setting establishes a context that reveals the circumstances and factors affecting the situation. It establishes a frame of reference that orients you to the context and gives you a way to approach the meaning of the dream.

I am standing inside a lobby in what appears to be a large resort hotel. Many people are running in a panic all around me.

From this first sentence, I know the dream is taking place in a public or collective setting where I am involved with many people who are afraid and panicking. This dream has something to do with my relationship to others rather than with my personal issues or complexes.

The setting in which your dreams take place can give you a clue about their personal, collective, or transpersonal context. A personal setting, such as a house or a room in a house, suggests the dream is related to your private life. You can explore such a dream in terms of what is going on in your personal psyche. A collective setting, such as a hotel lobby or an auditorium, suggests the dream is focusing on some social or public aspect of your life. In what way are you interfacing with the collective? A transpersonal setting, such as nature, the cosmos, a metaphysical or unfamiliar background, suggests some as yet unexplored creative or spiritual context.

The time frame of your dream is part of its setting. You can get a sense of the time frame by noticing the location and the characters in the dream. If they are from your past, the dream may be exploring an emotional issue from that time and place in your past that has become active in some way in your present life. If the time frame is now, for instance in your current home with people with whom you are presently involved, and with a plot that echoes something you are doing in your life, the dream is emphasizing the immediate importance of the dream message.

Some dreams take place in collective settings that suggest a time that is not possible for you to experience in your outer life. A setting such as a medieval dungeon, a space station, or some otherworldly or numinous mystical setting suggests a transpersonal dimension to the dream. Such completely unfamiliar settings suggest that something new needs to emerge or is emerging or is about to emerge in your awareness.

PLOTS

In addition to their physical setting, your dreams' dramatic structures occur in the context of other specific circumstances. The first stage of a dream story is the unfolding of the description of the initial situation in which the protagonist, the dream ego, has a conflict or problem with an antagonist. This element of story development is known in literature and also in dreams as the exposition. It presents an initial conflict that requires the characters to take some kind of action to affect the situation.

From above, where I'm floating, I observe men in camouflage uniforms shooting peo-
ple running across the grounds.

In the second stage, the dream story progresses, moving forward until
something favorable or unfavorable happens.

I am visible again [I stay rather than flee] . . . A man in a camouflage uniform
. . . tells us if we do not cooperate we will be killed.

In the third phase, the story reaches some sort of culmination in which
a resolution or another conflict occurs.

I am handed a loose-leaf book by a soldier and told to . . . show parents pictures of
their dead children.

In the fourth phase, the lysis, a solution or result, is revealed, or perhaps not.

The parents start to study the photographs . . . my phone rings, and I wake up.

When the solution is not revealed in a dream (and this is often the
case), the third phase is a good point of departure to continue writing
the dream forward in the process of visionary meditation we will discuss later.

When a dream is developed enough to have a series of scenes that
advance a plot, it means that your dreaming soul is trying to communicate some important and specific theme to your conscious self. When
the story is dynamic enough for you to realize a plot is unfolding, it suggests that you are ready to contemplate the theme and how it relates to
your life. Sometimes, a series of scenes that advance the plot occurs in
a single dream. Or a plot may often be advanced by a series of dreams.
The series may occur in one night, or a motif may repeat over a number of years. When the plot of one dream or a series of dreams has a

sequence of interrelated actions, they show what kind of conflict or resolution is going on between opposing forces in your psyche.

CHARACTERS

At a personal level, the characters in your dreams reflect various aspects of your personality and emotions. When the character is someone you do not know personally—like a celebrity—reflect upon the characteristics you associate with them. Do the same when the character is someone you know. The dream may or may not actually be about that person. Usually, the character is a way of bringing your attention to how you are acting or feeling like that character.

You may notice that certain dream characters make return appearances in your dreams. If you track them through a series of dreams, you can get a sense of an unfolding story that reflects some aspect of your unfolding development. The characters let you know if you are making progress, going backward, or spinning your wheels. Remember, these characters are always aspects of your own personality. When you repeatedly encounter a certain type, you are being asked to reflect on that aspect of your personality.

Your Dream Ego as Protagonist

The main character or protagonist in your dream drama is your dream ego—the character you recognize as yourself. Usually, your dream ego is the character playing the lead. Remember that usually, when your dream ego is acting in the dream, you are more likely to be at least somewhat consciously aware of the issue being presented in the dream. If your dream ego is separate and watching the action of the dream from a distance, that generally implies that you are still, to some extent, unconscious about that issue.

Your dream ego often plays a role that exaggerates or compensates for your conscious attitude. When your dream ego is in a "bigger-than-life" role in a dream, the message is usually that your external attitudes and behaviors are inflated. Or, conversely, the dream may be calling your attention to the fact that you are too passive or are allowing yourself to be victimized and deflated. Reflect upon each of these possibilities with an exaggerated dream that dramatizes an attitude or behavior. When your dream ego's role is special, unique, or extraordinary—whether that role is positive or negative—it is important to compare it to your conscious position.

A "bigger-than-life" dream may present a preview of a positive or negative potential that you have not yet discovered about yourself. Although it is difficult to do, it is important to reflect honestly about whether the dream is pointing to self-inflation or self-deflation within the context of a genuine potential or problem that is worthy of attention.

Following are two examples of exaggerated, inflated dreams. The first is a woman's dream, the second a man's.

I am standing on a stage in front of a large crowd of people. I am wearing a long flowing dress and my arms are raised toward heaven. The people in the crowd are bowing, cow-towing to me. As I raise my arms further toward heaven, I lift off the stage and fly above the crowd.

Of course, this may be a spiritual or transpersonal dream, but before the dreamer assumes it is revealing a call to lead others, it would be wise to look for shadow material. More benefit is likely to come from such a dream if it is explored first as though it were a dream from the personal realm of the shadow. This dreamer does so by exploring personal, family, and cultural associations to the above dream:

I have been reading and listening to tapes about spirituality lately. Maybe my ego would like to see me as one of the "enlightened" as opposed to one of the crowd. Perhaps my ego is trying to be the center of attention in my life in some way. Could be about my relationship with X. I was raised Catholic with all the delicious pomp and circumstance of the Mass. My family was very proud of being Catholic and considered themselves "above" non-Catholics. When I was a little girl, I felt I was special because I was a Catholic. I wanted to be a nun. I wanted to stay special. When I left the Catholic faith, I tried to be special by being an agnostic, then I considered myself to be an existentialist. I felt "better than" those who continued to believe in religion—the opiate of the masses. I was proud of being a nonreligious person, an intellectual who was not fooled by superstitious religions.

Considering these associations, the dreamer can discern a possible meaning in the dream:

This dream may be cautioning me to reconnect with my humility. Maybe I'm getting too egotistical and inflated in some aspect of my life.

An exaggerated dream that appears to be contradicting your attitude or behavior suggests that you should reflect on the theme from the opposite point of view in order to gain a more balanced perspective on your attitude. The following example of a man's dream and his personal, family, and cultural associations illustrates this point:

I am standing on a stage behind a podium. I am about to give a speech before a large audience. I put on my glasses and take a sip of water from the glass. I tap the microphone to make sure it is working. I arrange my notes in front of me. I look out over the audience and I know they are interested in my topic and I know the questions they are likely to ask. I have practiced what I will say so I am well prepared and confident.

The dreamer calls on the following associations to interpret the dream:

How odd. I can't imagine myself doing such a thing! I can't even speak well in front of two or three friends. I have been feeling critical of myself because I get tongue-tied. So critical that I usually avoid social situations where I might have to speak.

My mother wanted me to be a professional. I can remember when I was in grade school I was terrified to answer a question in class. I always spaced out. I was often embarrassed because I didn't hear the teacher's question. I would try to make up an answer, even though I didn't know what the question was, and it was always wrong. The other kids would laugh at me and I would want to disappear. Eventually my mother gave up and told me not to try so hard.

He ponders a possible meaning of the dream:

Perhaps I am more capable than I realize. Maybe I could be more comfortable with people if I felt more comfortable with myself and didn't worry so much about what other people think of me.

A dream often compensates for your awake behavior by suggesting an alternative. Dreams may show you acting dramatically in an unfamiliar and uncharacteristic manner that you cannot imagine happening in real life. You may awaken from such a dream feeling perplexed or with an "aha" experience of sudden insight. The sole purpose of even the worst nightmare is to correct some imbalance in your conscious attitude and help you function in a more healthy and creative way. Exercise 6 can help flesh out the role of your dream ego.

Exercise 6:
Fleshing Out Your Dream Ego Protagonist

Focus your intention on relaxing and meditating to turn your attention inward. While you are writing your dream, study your dream ego's behavior as you would pay attention to the main character in a story or movie. Notice the role you play. What are you doing? What is happening to you? How are you reacting? Notice if your dream-ego character behaves differently from or similar to your awake ego. Does it remain as a passive observer or does it participate in the dream action? Does it run or hide from danger, or does it confront the situation? Does it avoid challenges or does it take action?

◆ ◆ ◆

Dream Antagonists

Dream antagonists are similar to the antagonists in any drama. They support and challenge the main character, the dream ego and protagonist, in whatever situation is being enacted. They may be represented by a person or people that you know or that you do not know. They are whatever character in the dream is positively or negatively challenging your dream ego. They place some demand on your dream ego to resolve or integrate your relationship to the antagonistic element. This demand moves the storyline forward as your dream ego acts in response to the antagonist's character.

The antagonists in your dreams challenge and support the other actors in your dream story. If your dream ego has no antagonistic elements to react or relate to, nothing will happen in the story. Even a dream without other human characters, however, such as the second telepathic dream I related on page 29, will have some element in the setting, the situation, or the emotional experience that affects the dream ego and, therefore, the dreamer.

When you are an observer rather than a participating character in your dream, you are the protagonist. In that case, your dream ego and the content of the dream are both antagonists. Notice what happens in a dream story as a result of the way your dream ego interacts with the other characters and within the dream situation. Sometimes, just as in a novel, the resolution is blocked by some action or inaction of your dream ego or one of the other dream characters. Think about how the

action in the dream story helps you examine how you are stuck emotionally in some life situation.

As your various dream characters appear, the plot thickens. Each
character has some purposeful relationship to your conscious situation.
Each antagonist character in a dream represents some unfamiliar or
unwanted aspect of your own psyche. When you study how they act,
think, and feel, you learn how your unconscious psyche influences your
conscious personality.

Shadow Images

Sometimes the compensation or challenge from the dream is presented by the way an antagonistic character in the dream drama interacts with the protagonist dream ego. One such character in your
dreams is the shadow, which is traditionally the same gender as you
and often acts in a way that reflects some unrecognized negative or
dark side of your psyche.

The shadow is an archetype that is a key character in personal
dream work because "its nature can in large measure be inferred from
the contents of the personal unconscious."[1] The shadow takes forms
that reflect the parts of your psyche that are unknown to you or that
you avoid. The character playing the shadow may be someone you
know or a figure whom you do not know who illustrates a particular
personality trait. When you discover and integrate the shadow figures
in your psyche, you reveal the elements within your unconsciousness
that have a negative influence and that retard your development. In
order to develop your authentic self, you must recognize, accept, and
integrate the dark unwanted aspects of your personality.

We tend to project the unpleasant elements that show up in our
dreams onto people we find irritating and whom we judge or reject.
When you recognize and accept the negative shadow figures in your
dreams, you become less reactive to those same characteristics in other

people. This gives you a more objective and compassionate understanding of the realities of being human. The shadow character hidden behind the darkness of the negative shadow figure holds and reflects the positive potential to which you have not yet given form. When this begins to happen, the same-gender characters in your dreams may appear as teachers and mentors.

Negative shadow characters live in your dreams and in your life. As you become familiar with them in your dreams, your ability to recognize them in your life also increases. Although other people undoubtedly have shadow characteristics, the negative judgments you make about them are, at times, based on projections of your shadow material on them. On the other hand, sometimes such projections make people seem to be ideal friends or lovers and their shadow aspects are not seen. Then the person making the projection is also likely to be disillusioned. Exercise 7 can help you recognize negative shadow characters in dreams.

Exercise 7:
Antagonistic Shadow Characters

Focus your intention on relaxing and meditating to turn your attention inward. If you are a woman, think about the personality of the female characters in your dreams. If you are a man, think about the male characters. Ask: What is their emotional nature? What are their negative aspects? Are they seductive, violent, dishonest, deceptive, disgusting, or in any way repulsive or threatening to you? Write a description of their attitudes and behaviors. Reflect on and journal about the ways you may unconsciously be thinking, feeling, or acting the same way. Wonder in what area or relationships in your life you have negative emotional reactions to people or situations. Do you act more caring and supportive than you feel? Be willing to look for and acknowledge shadow aspects of your personality in order to recognize, acknowledge, and assimilate them.

◆ ◆ ◆

When you are able to identify the negative shadow elements of your personality, you are less emotionally reactive to them. When you are less emotionally reactive, you have accomplished a major step on your path to wholeness and individuation. As you recognize and relate to your shadow dream characters, you have a lifelong opportunity to become enlightened about yourself.

The following dream gives a sense of how to write associations to shadow dreams. Notice that the dream is written in the first-person, present-tense, fast-narrative style. The writing includes a possible interpretation for the dream. The man who wrote the example does a good job of using the subjective level of interpretation by thinking about images in the dream as symbols of various aspects of his personality. He is met by a shadow character and tries to understand in what way he is like that character by exploring personal, family, and cultural associations.

I am in a movie theater with people I don't know. The performance ends and I bend over and everything comes out of my pockets. By the time I pick stuff up, everybody has left. I go outside and I have no idea where I parked my car. I don't know if it is a familiar town. It reminds me of a local beach town. I walk and walk and walk. I decide that, since I cannot find the car, I will find a public phone. I go into a bar filled with black people. I am told the phone is in the bathroom. I go into the bathroom and search everywhere. There is no phone at all. I walk outside. Next to the bar is a cab station. I have money in my pocket so I can get a cab home and come back and search for my car tomorrow.

Somebody says: "You want a cab don't you? Let's decide what kind of cab you want. What do you want?" First he brings a Volvo; he spins the wheels and does 180-degree turns. He brings four different cars, different models and styles, and each time he changes his clothes and he is dressed up in a different outfit. I guess I figured out that this doesn't make any sense and I woke up.

The dreamer pulls associations from his dream and journals about them:

My family car is a Volvo. Most of the time, I do what my family likes. For example, I go to the theater, mostly to please them. I give up my personal preferences (the stuff in my pockets) when I bend over to please others. I get confused and out of touch with others (the crowd). I lose my personal authenticity and direction (my car). I am confused and cannot find my personal power (my car). I am not sure where I am (not a town I am familiar with). I go to an unfamiliar place where parts of my unconscious shadow self are gathered (bar with black people) to try to call for help (from my unconscious) but can't find a way to do so (the telephone). I can't get in touch with my own shadow (dark unconscious parts of my psyche). I try to use the conscious resources I have (money in my pocket) to get home (to a familiar place). The character who brings the cars is a shadow figure (same-gender dream character)—the part of me that keeps changing roles in my life to please others. I keep changing my persona, my image (the clothes), and the way I get what I want from people, my ego style (the cars) and that takes a lot of energy.

In my family, my father was a well-known public figure. He changed the way he acted depending on whether he was in front of a group or at home. I felt that he did not have time to be with me. I believed his work and the people in his congregation were more important to him than I was. I was sent to boarding school, and I had to learn how to get along with many different people. Then I was sent out of the country, and I had to learn to live with strangers.

He wonders about one possible meaning of the dream:

This dream may be suggesting I could pay more attention to the way I change to please people and lose touch with my personal preferences and authenticity. I could benefit from finding my authentic position and living my life from that awareness.

Invisible Dream Partners

Once you recognize and acknowledge the characters of your negative shadow, the next step in the individuation process is to come to terms with the opposite-gender aspects of your psyche. Traditional Jungian dream work includes the study of dream characters of the opposite gender. The male figures in a woman's dream (her *animus*) and the female figures in a man's dreams (his *anima*) teach the dreamer about the characteristics and qualities of the male or female aspects of his or her personality. The male and female characters develop and take on more depth and dimension in a series of dreams. The cast of characters crystallizes and then broadens to include many of the types found in life, in novels, and in movies.

The pendulum of psychological theory about what determines personality, intelligence, and behavior swings back and forth. Some models, like the medical model, declare that nature, or your genetic makeup, is completely responsible for the person you become. Other models, like the cognitive behavior model, state just as adamantly that nurture, or your environment, molds you into the person you are becoming. In Jung's model, the pendulum moves in a circle that integrates both and adds the essential elements of the collective, transpersonal and spiritual components of your psyche. Jung finds it empirically and experientially obvious that elements beyond heredity and environment influence human development. He believes our heritage includes trace memories of evolutions that are encoded in the collective unconscious. These trace memories appear in dreams as archetypal characters and situations, as in the following animus dream.

The following dream is from a woman who has a recurring nightmare that may be the result of childhood trauma. It illustrates the most primitive and negative level of the woman's animus figure. This woman's dream shows how dream writing and journaling can bring traumatic experiences and their resolution into conscious awareness.

I'm being followed by a tall, heavy man wearing a hat and dark clothes. I know he intends to harm me. I sense he will rape or kill me. I feel my heart pounding and my muscles tensing. I run and run and run for a long time until I finally come to my house. I get just inside the door and slam it a second before the man is able to push his way though the doorway. I lock the door and barricade it, first with my body and then with furniture. My heart is still racing as I run into the kitchen, pull a long butcher knife out of a drawer and hide behind the kitchen door. I wake up with my heart beating very fast and my right hand clenched. I am surprised to find I do not have a knife in my hand.

When this woman was a child, she was emotionally abused and physically beaten by her alcoholic stepfather. When he was not drinking, he was kind and playful with her, but when he was drinking, he became cruel. When she began dating, she tended to become emotionally involved with men who started out being kind and loving, but who turned mean and abusive when they drank alcohol. Even after she realized her pattern and only dated men who did not drink, she still found herself with men who seemed to change from being kind to being mean in the course of the relationship. She came to therapy because she wanted to have a healthy relationship. The barricade dream was the first one she had in therapy. Her subsequent dreams were often variations on the theme of barricading herself as a result of being pursued by a threatening man.

When a dream brings familiar and repetitive themes from the personal unconscious, it often refers to current life experiences that have not yet been reconciled and integrated. Although your attitudes toward the opposite sex are significantly influenced by your personal relationships with your opposite-sex parent, they are also deeply rooted in the collective unconscious. They may reflect genetic trace memories that seem unrelated to current life.

Exercise 8 can help to flesh out antagonistic characters of the opposite gender that play a role in your dreams. Remember, the key is to look for characteristics that may reflect attitudes or behaviors that you do not recognize on your own.

Exercise 8:
Antagonistic Anima and Animus Characters

Focus your intention on relaxing and meditating to turn your attention inward. Think and journal about the characters in your dreams and wonder how they represent, or are symbols for, some unconscious aspects of your personality. If the dream character is someone you know in your outer life, what do you think and feel about that character? What do you like or dislike about him or her? What positive or negative attributes do you associate with that character? How is that attribute present, but unacknowledged, in your behavior or attitude?

Ask: Who is participating in my dream? What are they doing? Do I know the other characters? If so, what is the personality of that person in my outer life? How are aspects of their personality present in my own actions or feelings at this time? Focus on any character that catches your attention or causes a strong emotional reaction. What in this character's nature draws your attention? What is your dominant impression of the character? How do the characters think, speak, and behave? What emotions are they feeling?

Try to connect each character to a specific situation in your life. Ask: What part of me is in that character or is in a similar type of situation? Where have I seen that character functioning in my life lately? Where and when do I see that same trait in my behavior? Who is it inside me who feels like that or behaves like that? How does that trait influence events and relationships in my life in a positive or negative manner?

◆　◆　◆

AMPLIFYING DREAMS
USING ASSOCIATIONS

The message in a dream can often be discerned by rereading the dream and including associations and amplifications to each element of the dream. Reflect on ways that the associations and amplifications give you some insight into how the dream relates to your current life.

Journaling about what you think the dream means, without being concerned about being right, can be helpful. Future dreams will repeat the necessary themes. If you pay attention to the repetition of themes over time, you will understand the message. This is the value of keeping a dream journal.

In the example below, the dreamer from page 85 adds her personal associations to the dream in parentheses, along with a statement of what she thinks the dream means about her personal growth. She had been working diligently to become aware of ways she acts in her life that set her up to be a victim. She began to recognize that she tended to feel threatened by people whom she thought of as more powerful, successful, or accomplished than she. Her work with the dream reflected this area of concern for her. She wanted to eliminate her tendency to take on the role of a victim in a variety of different relationships in her life. The process reflected in the following account is an example of amplification.

I'm (my dream ego) being followed by a tall, heavy man wearing a hat and dark clothes. (My stepfather or someone like him?) I know he intends to harm me. (He has in the past.) He will rape or kill me. (He has violated me.) I feel my heart pounding and my muscles tensing. (My body is feeling my fear.) I run and run and run, for a long time (I have avoided my father for ten years) until I finally come to my house (I had to get my own strong ego). I get just inside the door and slam it a second before the man pushes his way inside. (I am getting stronger just in time!) I lock the door and barricade it (I know my clear boundaries now), first with my body (at first I have to use my body to keep him away) and then with furniture (as I get stronger I have other resources to protect myself). My heart is still racing (I am still afraid of him). As I run into the kitchen (I go to a place to nurture myself and find more strength), I pull a long butcher knife out of a drawer (I find power to defend myself) and hide behind the kitchen door (I can be a predator if I need to). I wake up with my heart beating very fast and my right hand clenched in a tight fist. I am surprised to find I do not have a knife in my hand. (Whew that felt very real!)

She reflects on one possible message of the dream:

I feel better about taking care of and fighting for myself. I am getting stronger, but I am still afraid and on the run.

If, when you speculate about the meaning of a dream, your interpretation is incorrect, the correction may come in another dream. Or some event in life may bring attention to the theme of the dream. You may realize, for example, that you are using a lot of energy to cope with a situation or person. Jung suggested that people unconsciously act out unresolved issues by manifesting them in their lives. When you reflect upon and make an effort to make sense of and find solutions for the problems and misfortunes in your life, you learn from them. If you ignore or deny them, they recur until you resolve them or are defeated by them. As you attempt to resolve a situation, a dream or a series of dreams often contributes metaphors that help clarify the meaning. With that said, it is also true that over-interpretation can take the spirit and energy out of a dream. It is often helpful to live with a dream and allow insight and understanding to unfold while mulling it over or writing it forward in the state of visionary meditation.

key in the door and open it. (I am successful in finding the tools I need to take care of myself.) Then I turn around and see a man standing a few feet away in the shadows (I can face the reality of what my father did to me). I say very loudly, (I have my voice!) "If you hurt me, you will have to kill me because I will die fighting you." The man turns and walks away. (I confront him at last; it is him or me and I mean it!) The man turns and walks away. (Hooray!)

She ponders this possible interpretation:

I know life is not this simple, but I can feel that I am so much stronger and less intimidated than I used to be. I speak up for myself more, even when I am afraid. Good for me!

When she turned and confronted her fear in the dream, this woman felt more objective and confident that she could have a clear and strong position about her authentic self and her boundaries in her relationships. She could choose a healthier partner, and could be a healthier partner.

A successful resolution in a dream amplifies and supports your conscious attitude or compensates for it by suggesting a way to achieve resolution. Dream dramas show how you cope with your raw emotions. The way your dream ego copes in a dream shows you how effective or ineffective your coping skills are and may suggest ways to improve them. Exercise 10 will help you gain experience in fleshing out a dream and exploring your associations for its possible meaning.

Exercise 10:
Making Associations to a Dream

Choose a dream that you have written in first-person, present-tense, fast-narrative style and practice fleshing it out. Focus your intention on relaxing and meditating to turn your attention inward. Describe your emotions

Exercise 9:
Living with a Dream

Focus your intention on relaxing and meditating to turn your attention inward. Once you have written your dream, rather than trying to interpret it immediately, mull it over, carry it around with you, live with it inwardly and ask questions of it. Be aware of what is going on in your outer life that may remind you of the dream. Look for aspects of the dream that remind you of things that show up in your outer life. Perhaps an experience, a song, a story, or a movie resonates with your dream. Make a note of anything that seems related to the dream. It is perfectly fine if your associations change. You may feel that the dream has one message when you first reflect on it, then find later that you feel it has a different message. Trust your intuition to guide you. Let yourself speculate. Don't worry about being right. Dreams are self-correcting. If you don't quite "get it" with one dream, another will come along to clarify the issue. This is a way to continue to weave your dreams into a consistent tapestry of meaning.

◆ ◆ ◆

Each time you experience a sense of the meaning of a dream, you become more sophisticated in your ability to understand the messages of future dreams. A dream that supports your interpretation of a past dream can do so in a very direct and clear manner. The same woman whose dream we just explored had the following dream, which seems to support her interpretation and her personal growth.

I am walking across a college campus to my car. (I am stronger, on my own two feet, getting smarter and I have the power to get around). It is dark. (I am no longer afraid of the dark.) I hear footsteps behind me. I walk faster and the footsteps speed up, too. (I recognize potential danger and I take action.) I come to my car, put my and the sensory experiences of the dream. Continue to brainstorm and journal about how the dream is symbolic of an experience in your present or past life.

What does the dream remind you of? What does it lead you to think about in your personal life? Write your associations and thoughts in first-person fast-narrative style.

◆　◆　◆

As you become familiar with the quality and meaning of personal dreams, your dream-writing process will result in healing. What you learn and the changes you feel as a result of personal dream writing can increase your ability to recognize your collective and transpersonal dreams. These dreams have a dramatic structure of mythic proportions. As you continue writing your dreams, the characters in those dreams will introduce you to the power of the archetypes.

5

fleshing out
collective and
transpersonal
dreams

*Magician and demon are mythological figures which express the
unknown, "inhuman" feeling. . . . They are attributes not in any sense
applicable to a human personality. . . . These attributes always indicate that
contents of the transpersonal or collective unconscious are being projected.*

—C. G. JUNG, *CW* 7, ¶ 149–150

While many dreams seem to be about the realm of personal experiences, some dreams are about collective and/or transpersonal
experiences. And some dreams are combinations of the two. Once you
attend to your dreams for their relevance to your personal life, you can
go on to explore them in terms of their collective and transpersonal
significance.

Jung thought of the collective transpersonal unconscious as "a
deeper layer of the unconscious where the primordial images common
to humanity lie sleeping."[1] Collective dreams tend to reflect your relationship with the traditional beliefs and notions of your personal

family, social group, and the larger group we call humanity. Some of them will have familiar themes; some will not. The archetypes in these dreams echo the genetic memory and history of human experience and imagination.

Transpersonal dreams reflect a deeper dimension beyond the collective psyche. They are more numinous, metaphysical, preternatural, and spiritual than personal and collective dreams. They present images and stories of what you experience as sacred, essential, and divine universal energies. They show up as mythical, philosophical, and religious dramas with archetypal characters that shape and inspire you to spiritual aspirations and creative discovery. Transpersonal dreams are transcendental; they germinate in the deepest level of your unconscious psyche.

Psychologically, to be unconscious means to be unaware. That means that, at any moment in which you are focused on one thing, you are unconscious or not aware of anything else that is stored in your psyche. That includes all that you have experienced and are not focused on, and all that you know intuitively or through your genetically evolved memory, but have not yet integrated into consciousness.

The unconscious part of your psyche is constantly and actively involved in processing what it knows and transmitting that knowledge to your conscious ego to increase your conscious awareness. The deep levels of your psyche are always actively processing the contents of the collective unconscious. This relatively active state means that the essential energy of your unconscious is a vital and influential component of your psyche—one that you apprehend through the archetypes in your dreams.

THE NATURE OF MIND

One way to clarify the basic underlying energy of archetypes in dreams is to explore the nature of the mind that exists beyond the neurological and biochemical components of the brain. There are many philosophical, psychological, and spiritual models that speculate on the nature of the mind. For instance, all the teachings and practices of Tibetan Buddhism focus on seeking truth and understanding inside the nature of the mind, rather than outside in the world. The true nature of the mind, according to Tibetan Buddhism, is called *rigpa*, which Sogyal Rinpoche describes thus:

> Imagine a sky, empty, spacious, and pure from the beginning; its *essence* is like this. Imagine a sun, luminous, clear, unobstructed, and spontaneously present; its *nature* is like this. Imagine that sun shining out impartially on us and all things, penetrating all directions; its *energy*, which is the manifestation of compassion, is like this: Nothing can obstruct it, and it pervades everywhere.[2]

William James, in *The Varieties of Religious Experience* describes mind as a multiplicity of basic and essential qualities within human consciousness and spiritual experiences. The field of consciousness, James says,

> . . . lies around us like a "magnetic field" inside of which our center of energy turns like a compass needle as the present phase of consciousness alters into its successor. Our whole past store of memories floats beyond its margin, ready at a touch to come in; and the entire mass of residual powers, impulses, and knowledge that constitute our empirical self stretches continuously beyond it. So vaguely drawn are the outlines between what is actual and what is only potential at any moment of our conscious life, that it is always hard to say of certain mental elements whether we are conscious of them or not.[3]

Indian and Tibetan mystics who documented the existence of a luminous energy field thousands of years ago described it as an aura or halo around the physical body. Ancient cultures refer to a field of energy that surrounds the physical body and informs it just as a magnet organizes the filings on a piece of glass. This energy field, which surrounds the Earth, is an electromagnet field that extends into space, indeed "to the edge of the universe."[4]

Western culture defines the human soul as immaterial, incorporeal energy that exists without a physical body; it views it as part of the psyche. From this point of view, your soul is the instigating and vital principle within your psyche that senses, intuits, thinks, and feels. Your dreaming soul is an aspect of this vital energy that infuses and informs your dreams, visionary meditations, and other altered states of awareness. It cannot be tangibly located within your physical senses, but it can be experienced. Jung calls the soul ". . . a psychic activity that transcends the limits of consciousness."[5] This independent entity, whether it is designated as the Self, the soul, or the dreaming soul, is the creative imaginative aspect of your psyche that you access through dream writing. This connection is promoted through a combination of emotional, psychological, and numinous spiritual dreams and meditative experiences that guide you toward individuation and self-realization.

INDIVIDUATION AND SELF-REALIZATION

The collective transpersonal unconscious influences and interfaces with your individuation process. As you become mindful of some of the contents of your unconscious psyche, you integrate what you learn into your daily life. Individuation means becoming an individual, and, in so far as individuality is an expression of your innermost and incomparable uniqueness, it also implies becoming your authentic self. Individuation means coming to selfhood, or self-realization.

Your progress toward self-realization is influenced by your growing ability to focus and shift your awareness from literal ordinary experiences to symbolic, mythic, and essential-energy experiences. Psychic energy from your unconscious inspires, stimulates, activates, and enlightens you. Your thoughts, feelings, and behaviors are influenced by your unconscious psyche and vice versa, even though, most of the time, you probably don't realize it.

Your dreams are created from experiences and memory traces in your conscious and unconscious psyche. When they are assimilated, they help you integrate those memories and experiences in a way that leads to individuation, self-realization, and increased consciousness. The core of these experiences is available through contact with your dreams and with the deeper levels within and beyond your psyche. Your intention and attention to your dreams affects what you experience consciously and what remains unconscious to you.

Although, theoretically, you can never experience the full content of your unconscious psyche, some mystics and explorers of altered states of consciousness have had experiences during which they apprehend "something," perhaps a sort of universal psychic energy that exists and cycles through the microcosm of their individual psyche and the macrocosm, the "all-that-is" of creation. That "something" is the inspiration of poets, metaphysicians, and other creative people.

Archetypes as Mentors

Dream-writing practice helps you connect with this universal psychic energy through the archetypal forces in your dreams that unconsciously influence your physical, emotional, mental, and spiritual development. As you discover and recognize these forces, you become aware of their influence on your thoughts, feelings, and actions. As you assimilate and integrate them, you become stronger and more creative.

You meet your mentor archetypes as the inner gurus that connect you with the instinctive divine spark of your authentic Self. These experiences are enlightening, which, in a Western sense, means to have both intellectual understanding and spiritual insight. Literal and intellectual understanding is valuable, but not enough. Insight happens when you reflect on a dream as a metaphor that refers to your inner truths and possibilities. In time, such reflection creates a dynamic connection with the wisdom of your mentor archetypes.

Jung describes the mentor archetype as "a distinctly numinous character [that is] 'spiritual,' if 'magical' is too strong a word . . . healing or destructive, but never indifferent [it appears] in the form of a *spirit* [that sometimes] comports itself like a ghost."[6] Numinous characters have an immortal, everlasting quality about them. James Hillman refers to such archetypes as "the deepest patterns of psychic functioning, the roots of the soul governing the perspective we have of ourselves and the world."[7]

The archetypal roots that appear in your dreams, imaginative fantasies, and visionary meditations are core images and ideas that represent your intuitive wisdom. They reveal the intrinsic, innate forces that inspire your life. These forces are shown directly to you through your dream experiences. They are your inner truth. They are unquestionably authentic, because they come from your psyche and your connection with divine wisdom.

Archetypes feel more important than ordinary dream-life characters. They are numinous, visionary beings that guide you on self-reflective experiences toward individuation. They appear in dreams that are outside and beyond your usual frame of reference. Notice the role of the archetypes in this dream.

I'm kneeling in the sand, wet sand, a shoreline. Apparently the tide is out. Another person is kneeling facing me. I am looking down at what at first appears to be a fat spiral-shaped shell protruding from the wet sand. It is about 1½ inches long and an inch wide. I am enthralled by the shape, color, and pattern. The shape seems particularly familiar. The colors are shades of blue and green and sand that add contour and depth to the shell. As I study the shell, I begin to see that it slopes out on either side just below the surface of the sand. I lean down to look more closely. My eye follows a shape just under the sand that extends out toward the sea. I ask the figure in front of me to move away because it is kneeling on part of it. I follow the form that extends out from the shell; it looks like a face under the sand. The shell is actually the nose of a male figure. I see the cheeks and well-formed full lips. The eyes are closed. The contours of the face are in perfect alignment. I follow the form under the sand to the shoulders and the right arm. I sense this man is going to open his eyes and, indeed, his eyelids begin to move slightly. I am excited and a little scared. This is the Green Man! I look around for RS. I see him back in a crowd of people on the beach. I wave and catch his eye and gesture for him to come quickly. He waves and continues what he is doing, indicating he will be here in a minute. I am impatient. I want him to validate my impression that this is the Green Man and I don't want him to miss what is happening. So I get up, look down at the Green Man and decide he won't open his eyes right away. I turn around and walk back to RS. I tell him it is important that he come see something right away. He says okay and leisurely gets up. I start back toward the Green Man with RS following me.

Then, the Green Man is up and out into the blue like a small tornado. The whirlwind spirals into the sky, turns and fires a burst of flame at the crowd on the ground. People start running and yelling. RS and I are looking up. RS says "Yep, it's the Green Man." We grin at each other. I don't know what will happen. The scene is now more like a city with high-rise buildings. I am afraid that the Green Man is probably going to wreak havoc on this city.

Let's consider the events in my life that surrounded this dream. The night before, a group of us had burned a fire stick to Pacamama for the healing of the Earth. As the "crone" of the group, I placed the fire stick into the fire. I blew into the stick my intention to release fear of anything that interfered with my creative expression along with the group's intention to heal the earth. As I did so, I saw an image of transformation, of the decomposition of all that is pollution and destroying nature. Then I saw a resolution of destruction and the rebirth of the organic process. It was a brief but powerful vision, like a dust cloud of energy, with blue and green and gold and a little bit of red sparks of energy swirling in a spiral pattern. WB lifted it up along a burning piece of wood. Instead of bursting into flames, it shriveled and curled and moved like a serpent. It split in half and each half undulated as a separate serpent. We each recognized that and commented on it at the same time. The serpent is a symbol of death, of the past and rebirth, of what is possible. It is a symbol of transformation. So I evoked the decomposition energy.

The Green Man is a mythological archetype associated with the fecund cycle of life on Earth.[8] In this dream, there is danger to the collective. The Green Man rises up out of the earth, out of the sand at the edge of the sea (the unconscious), takes to the sky, and turns on the people in the middle of a city, breathing flame upon the industrial pollution (city life) that is destroying nature. There is no green earth in the city. As cities sprawl over the globe, the Green Man is pushed farther and farther out of his primordial responsibility for the fecund procreation of life on Earth. I had recently been out of touch with the Earth, with my relationship to it, and with my own groundedness because I had been so focused on writing and on personal relationships. In the dream, however, I was not afraid. "The Green Man has returned as the living face of the whole earth so that through his mouth we may say to the universe: 'We are one.'"[9] The danger was not personal, but it would affect me as part of the collective. RS symbolized the Green Man in the sense that he was interested in that archetype and because he is a defender of the Earth. As an animus symbol in this dream, he (I) had the strength to see the value in the destruction and decomposition. So the dream caused me to reflect on how I was neglecting my relationship to nature and how I am participating in a natural, organic reality.

When you become aware of a numinous dream, one that is clearly beyond ordinary experience, you feel and know that you are traveling with the archetypes, the ancient ones. Such a dream often lingers, wafting in and out of your waking awareness. An archetypal character has sufficient energy to take a powerful form and to stay present in your conscious memory. It may show up as a mentor, healer, mystical being, or evil daemon. It may appear as an ancient character like the Green Man who looks or acts like a powerful individual from literature, history, religion, or mythology.

Collective or transpersonal archetypes are often unfamiliar, extraordinarily powerful, and numinous. You may experience archetypes through any or all of your physical senses. You may see them, feel them touch your body, hear their voices, smell them, even taste them. They may make love to you or try to strangle you. They manifest in your dreams as tangible, physical, and emotional experiences that have a numinous quality that can be difficult to describe or define. They come to you in your dreams as mysterious beings that take your breath away or breathe new life into your soul.

Your mentor archetypes offer you opportunities to reflect on yourself and change. They reflect and teach you about your own collective and transpersonal depth. Although many of these archetypes can be found in myths, legends, and religions throughout human history, Jung emphasizes that their meaning is particular to the individual dreamer.[10] In other words, your dreaming soul presents the archetypes in dream stories that will best dramatize what is relevant to you and the state of your interior world.

Because an archetype is an ancient primeval representation of human experience, it takes form in a dream as contact with "the other." You feel as if you have been visited by an intangible being that is strangely familiar and yet frustratingly obscure. It may appear as a character, an atypical situation, or a strong sensual or emotional experience that expresses itself symbolically and metaphorically and is affected by your particular temperament. Collective and transpersonal dreams put you in contact with the source of your essential creative energy because they connect you with the universe of possibilities that exists beyond what you think you know about reality. Often that connection is made with the help of mentors that show up in your dreams.

Remember Michael, the carver of Celtic myths? His story lingers in my memory like such a dream, hinting at the mysterious quality of transpersonal experiences. Michael had been a butcher before he became a wood carver. Pointing to a symbol on the back of his Night Hawk carving, he told me it was the *Sobar cu'*, a "dark, wet depth hound that lives in the shadowy pool"—a symbol well-known in North Connacht. I looked closely at the spiral image, which had large eyes and an open mouth with an extended tongue.

There are many Irish stories in which the hound from the dark depths plays the adversary, the tester. Usually young women and men encounter and are challenged or threatened by the Sobar cu'. Strangely enough, the advice hidden in the stories seems to be, "When the hound appears, run like hell!" This is not panic-stricken flight, however, because the fleer seeks help—from a human friend, the natural world, an animal spirit, or convenient earth work. The key is that you must never freeze. You must seek help to understand your adversary and use that understanding to develop the power of wisdom.

Above the hound, Michael pointed to another spiral shape in the form of a fish. It held something I could not recognize, which Michael identified as the *Brasan Feasa*, the "salmon of wisdom," which gets its power from the dark depth hound, the adversary. The salmon feeds in the dark depths and then leaps out, fat and full of the wisdom that comes from the underworld. Jung offers one possible interpretation of the fish symbol in a dream: "it is the 'nourishing' influence of the unconscious contents, which maintain vitality of consciousness by continual influx of energy; for consciousness does not produce its energy by itself."[11] In some sense, when you are waking from a dream, you are running like hell from the Sobar cu', the dark depths of your unconsciousness. When that happens, you may wonder if you will make it back through the door that has opened to something beyond ordinary reality. As you wake from such a dream, you are, in a sense, running toward another door, the door that will return you to the outer world of light, rational understanding, and conscious awareness. If you stay calm and don't panic, you can remain aware of your dreaming experience and bring it back with you. If you remember the dream, you have the opportunity to remember and re-experience where you were when you went beyond ordinary reality. Then you can journey and journal through the dream material for insight and wisdom.

From out of your depths, the shadow of your private dark, wet Sobar cu' hound challenges you to face what lives in the unlit places of your psyche. Soulful dream writing helps you transform the raw energy of your dreams into refined meaning and energy that you can direct toward your life purpose. You are empowered to develop your life and creative expression.

It is common, however, to let a dream fall back into the soup, into the indistinct depths of your unconscious. When I'm tired, sleepy, or simply not in the mood, I don't want to explore what is waiting in the darkness. I have learned, however, to accept and even value the occasional discomfort of staying in touch with these dreams. It is worth tolerating because of the insight and understanding they offer me.

The glimpses that archetypes give you into the nature of your personal, collective, and transpersonal memory traces can change your life. When you realize the potent possibilities of these dreams, you are more inclined to make the effort to explore them as you move closer to the edge of the unfamiliar. It is here, at what William James calls "the fringes of consciousness" and beyond that you find the essential energy to heal and reach your creative potential.

Often, as I awaken from a dream, the boundary between the dream and my waking experience is unclear. I feel as though, while I was dreaming, I was physically present and participating in some other dimension of reality. As I awake from such a dream, I feel a bit disoriented and perhaps even disappointed (or relieved) to discover that the experience was only a dream. These feelings are a sign to me that the dream is meaningful, even if it is not easy to understand in terms of literal reality. Perhaps, while dreaming, I have touched that fringe of consciousness and a new archetypal truth has come alive. In this sense, the mentor archetypes in my dreams teach me what I need to become aware of in order to create and change.

"The karmic factor is essential to a deeper understanding of the nature of an archetype."[12] When I began studying Hindu and Buddhist thought, I mistook the concept of karma for punishment, like the Catholic doctrine of purgatory. I imagined that we accumulated karma in proportion to our sins. I thought that the various lifetimes of suffering must be like purgatory and that, by suffering, we would burn away the karma of those sins.

Since then, I have come to a deeper understanding of the concept. Sogyal Rinpoche observes that karma "is not fatalistic or predetermined. Karma means our ability to create and to change. It is creative because we *can* determine how and why we act."[13] Thus it follows that, when my ability to make conscious choices to change and recreate my future is limited, my karma or creative imagination needs attention. I can affect the karma of my ordinary mind with its habits and projections through compassionate self-reflection. I can create a conscious intention to change my negative patterns of thought, feeling, and behavior. In this way, I can invite new archetypes to appear.

Big Dreams and Archetypes

A big dream, like Storm Troopers or The Green Man, feels pregnant with numinosity and unborn creative potential. The role you play in such a dream activates an intense emotional response and takes you beyond your ordinary life experience. The suspense and quality of dramatic mythic energy pulls you into the action of the dream and into other dimensions of reality that exist beyond your everyday experiences. Jung describes big dreams as significant dreams that "are often remembered for a lifetime, and not infrequently prove to be the richest jewel in the treasure-house of psychic experience."[14]

Because big dreams often contain energy that is fundamentally essential to consciousness, they have a visionary, mysterious aura. They seem to defy any attempt at rationalization. When you awaken from such a numinous archetypal dream, you feel the lingering presence of its vital energy. A powerful, inspiring presence remains that leaves a deep impression on your thoughts, feelings, and body. Such dreams often result in profound changes in your attitudes about personal and spiritual values. They broaden your awareness of the universal and collective human community.

Although your dreaming soul originates dreams using unconscious memories and often casts the dream ego as the protagonist in the leading role, it also draws on your outer life to inform the dream and provide external points of reference. When unconscious dream material is blended with conscious awareness, something new is revealed. The new discovery helps you develop the ability to integrate and digest the paradoxes in life, solve problems, develop personal and spiritual insight, and give form to your creative imagination.

Archetypal Dream Antagonists

Your dream ego often appears as the protagonist in collective and transpersonal dreams, and meets powerful antagonistic characters that are the catalysts for profound change. Personal dream antagonists may be the images of recognizable people. Collective and transpersonal dream antagonists may also be familiar, but are often archetypal figures that appear as humans, animals, spirits, images like the Green Man, or essential energy experiences. They may be forces of nature such as wind, hurricanes, tornados, rain, floods, avalanches, earthquakes, explosions, and fires that represent the four basic elements of air, water, earth, and fire.

When an antagonistic archetypal character such as the Green Man is extremely numinous, it tends to represent the shadow of the collective or transpersonal unconscious. It feels dangerous and threatening in a larger and less personal sense, because it typically represents the collective and transpersonal shadow, or the dark side of society and human consciousness. It may appear as a mob, murderer, rapist, or robber, or it may show up as demonic, evil, or powerfully destructive characters.

However, such characters also reflect aspects of the collective shadow that are present in you as unconscious potential for destruction and violence. They suggest the need to face your anger and fear and step into the consciousness of the luminous warrior who takes his or her share of responsibility for the collective shadow.

When numinous characters are positive, they appear in whatever form is most inspiring to you, such as benevolent and virtuous characters like shamanic healers or illuminating angels. When they are negative, they appear in whatever form is most intimidating to you. Exercise 11 can help you explore the archetypal characters in your dreams.

Exercise 11:
Dream Work with Archetypes

Look for an example of an archetype in a dream—a character like the Green Man that feels bigger than ordinary reality and causes you to have an emotional response in your dream. Focus your intention on relaxing and meditating to turn your attention inward. Reflect on what that archetype's characteristics symbolize to you in your personal life. Journal about how you react to that archetype's characteristics when they show up in your relationships and in the various roles you play in your outer life. By deepening your understanding of each archetype in your dreams and journaling about how they may be influencing your life, you lessen their unconscious power and you can make more aware choices. Ask: Why is this archetype in my dream at this time? How does it represent some aspect of my life? How does the archetype present me with an opportunity for a deeper understanding of myself and others? How does the archetype present me with an opportunity to develop latent abilities and talents? How does it call my attention to a situation or attitude that I need to change or develop? Are the characters in my dream part of the history, myths, or religious and cultural beliefs in my family? If so, what do they symbolize for my development?

◆ ◆ ◆

Anima and Animus Archetypes

In addition to the shadow aspects of your psyche, you will also encounter various dream characters of the opposite gender in collective and transpersonal dreams. These dream partners are invisible to conscious awareness. As we learned in chapter 4, they are inner expressions of the opposite-gender energy within you and are referred to in Jungian terms as anima (female soul in men) and animus (male spirit in women).

In personal dreams, these archetypes may appear as people you recognize. In collective and transpersonal dreams, they are characters that are experienced as bigger than life, like the Green Man. They reflect the level of development of your contra-sexual attitudes and potentials.

The symbolism of these contra-sexual images can be obscure and difficult to grasp at first. But when you track them in their various developmental stages, you learn to understand what they represent in a dream.
As you become familiar with various aspects of these archetypes, they
become tangible and familiar allies, rather than unconscious influences.

You can think of the anima and animus as having stages of development.

> The first stage [of a man's animus] . . . represents purely
> instinctual and biological relations. The second . . . personifies
> a romantic and aesthetic level that is . . . characterized by sex-
> ual elements. The third is . . . a figure who raises love (eros) to
> the heights of spiritual devotion. The fourth type is . . . wis-
> dom transcending even the most holy and the most pure. . . . A
> woman's animus appears [first] as a personification of mere
> physical power . . . [then] he possesses initiative and the capac-
> ity for planned action. . . . [then] becomes the "word," often
> appearing as a professor or clergyman. Finally, [he] is the incar-
> nation of meaning. . . . He gives the woman spiritual firmness,
> an invisible inner support that compensates for her outer
> softness.[15]

These stages of transformation through which the inner, contra-sexual
figures pass are part of the ongoing process of individuation. Indeed,
you can learn about your own personal development by being aware of
and tracking the development of your opposite-gender archetypes.
These archetypal characters show you where you are on your developmental path. As inner mentors and allies, they lead the way along the
path to individuation. They are not always friendly; in fact, they can be
absolutely terrifying. The following is an example of a transpersonal
antagonistic archetype in a dream I had about ten years ago. The dream
character was so numinous I felt his physical presence.

I am lying in bed, asleep. I sense a presence in the room and, suddenly, a big man is looming over me; he hisses "Shut up" as he grabs me. His face is very close to mine. He places his hand around my throat. I take in a sudden deep breath and try to call out for my father. I try to get the words out before this man's hands close on my throat. My eyes pop open and I see the man. He is about thirty, tall and large, with short dark hair and a craggy, pock-marked face. I don't recognize him. I am disoriented for a while. It is clear he means to harm me. He is mean.

My heart is racing. Then I realize my eyes are actually open and I am in my own room. I can hear my dog breathing and I remind myself that I am safe and that no one can be in the room because she would have barked. I calm myself, trusting she will protect me. I would be more uncertain about reality without her.

When I close my eyes, the man is still present, I feel his hands on my throat. I see his eyes staring into mine. I am terrified, yet calm. I think that I should keep my eyes closed and go through whatever is going to happen. I slowly open and close my eyes several times. His presence fades a little more each time, and then he is gone. I stay in bed wondering where he came from. How could he be just a dream when he was so real? I could feel his breath on my face. The dream was quite lucid. After a while, when he does not reappear when I close my eyes, I get up and walk around the room. I am alone, my dog is sleeping, but I feel as though the man has just left the room.

Whew! What a night! The attack was scary, not only because such a thing happened, but because it felt as if it were really happening. It was reminiscent of the dark man pursuing me in dreams I had when I started analysis. What personal associations did the dream hold for me? Why is the "strong, dangerous man" animus back at this time? It seems like old stuff. It is the undeveloped animus, for sure, but at a more numinous level than in my early dreams. What about my current life reflects that energy? Perhaps this is an exaggeration to bring my attention to a way in which I am being strangled in my relationship. Usually, when my dreams regress and reduce me to encountering my primitive destructive animus, I am either doing something in my life that is setting me up to be exploited, or I am feeling destructive toward someone. But this was so violent. I can't find a current situation in which I might be so victimized or so angry toward someone. Something is stirring the old dark stuff in me, old fears about being victimized and harmed by men. I'll watch for where this energy is in my life and pay attention to what future dreams bring.

What archetypal associations does the dream convey? Certainly the dream is a re-enactment of the archetype of the evil predator. The character in this dream is a killer, without conscience or compassion— a true representative of the dark side. Perhaps, since this character is so numinous, he represents a collective archetype of the patriarchal strangulation of the feminine. In that case, my dreaming soul gives me a personal experience of being strangled by the man in my dream in order to call my attention to the presence of that oppression in the collective. But I am well aware of that, so why is it being emphasized now? How is that present in my life and what can I do about it? I'll watch for this, too.

My strong emotional response in this dream is obviously a reductive signal to pay attention. In what way am I out of touch with the energy that the dream stirs? In response to the dream, I decide to watch for how I may be ignoring such dark energy in my personal life and in the collective. Perhaps I am being naive and denying the possibility of emotional or physical danger in my life. Perhaps I am using denial because I am frightened and unable to cope with the possibility of hurt or loss. If I pay attention to the dream and remain alert, but not paranoid about possible danger, I will be more likely to take appropriate precautions and may prevent me or someone else from being harmed in some way.

Your Invisible Dream Partner

The level of development of your invisible dream partner (the opposite-gender character in your dreams) suggests whether or not a dream is related to issues stemming from your personal or the collective transpersonal unconscious. If the character acts in ways that reflect an early, more primitive, stage of development, the dream is more likely to be concerned with ego or personal development. When the character is bigger than life and acts in ways that reflect a more conscious stage of development, the dream is more likely to be concerned with the development of the Self. To become acquainted with the opposite gender characters in your dreams, try Exercise 12.

Exercise 12:
Discovering Your Invisible Partner

Focus your intention on relaxing and meditating to turn your attention inward. If you are a woman, study the personality of opposite-gender figures in your dreams. Where do you place them in the developmental sequence described on page 108? How does the part they play, the way they act, in your dream reflect your experience with men in your life? Include your father, brothers, uncles, and all men who have had a significant positive or negative impact on your life. Remember stepfathers, stepbrothers, boyfriends, teachers and neighbors, even strangers who may have impacted you emotionally. How is that influence still active in your present life?

If you are a man, study the style of the opposite-gender figures in your dreams. Where would you place them in the developmental sequence? How does the part they play, the way they act, in your dream reflect your experience with women in your life? Include your mother, sisters, grandmothers, aunts, and all women who have had a significant positive or negative impact on your life. Remember step-mothers, stepsisters, girlfriends, teachers, and neighbors. How is that influence still active in your present life?

◆　◆　◆

My friend Jan Freya expresses her understanding of the development of the animus characters in her dreams:

> It was important to me to understand that a certain dream fig-ure can reflect varying stages of animus development in rela-tion to different situations in our lives. Mine seem to appear as more or less developed in different situations—not always advancing toward the more developed levels. Maybe the poten-tial for any level of manifestation of animus/anima is always there, related to the developmental process of the ego, or ego strength that differs with the challenge we face as we gain mas-tery of different areas of our life. Sometimes our animus is an ineffectual baby and sometimes a hero, depending on what we're facing.

It is eye-opening to recognize how conditioning about the opposite gender, as well as the perceptions or reactions that have been inherited from collective memories, affect the quality of relationships. They also impact your capacity to recognize your ability to manifest the healthy aspects that are usually attributed to the opposite sex.[16] It is also useful to develop your opposite-gender qualities to round out your full poten-tial and personality. The relationship between the inner masculine and feminine aspects of your psyche leads toward individuation. Once you are able to recognize dream images that represent the shadow aspects of your personality, you can also focus on the opposite-gender aspects of your personality, your invisible partners. As you integrate all these inner aspects of your psyche, you feel yourself grow and change. Once you can recognize, understand, accept, and assimilate the various aspects of your psyche, you understand and accept yourself. The excitement that comes with integrative change releases the flow of creative energy and opens the possibility for transpersonal development.

TRANSPERSONAL DEVELOPMENT, DREAMS, AND THE EGO

We are each capable of developing a transpersonal identity that can transcend the personal ego and experience levels of awareness beyond ordinary reality. Transcendental insights are part of many religious experiences. But they were first included in the field of psychology when Jung wrote about the transcendent function as the ability to integrate the paradox of opposite realities and discover something new. This ability is developed by reflecting on contradictory experiences and images that lead to an "Aha" insight. Such an experience helps you evolve and function at levels of consciousness that are not completely bound by the needs of your personal ego. When your awareness extends beyond personal gratification, your ego is healthy and works in cooperation with your soul toward the development of your higher Self.

Dream writing and journaling is one way to develop the transcendent function because the process helps you reflect on and endure the tension of the opposing realities you experience within yourself, until some new insight emerges. You evolve this transcendent function by experiencing, surviving, and integrating contradictions, ambiguities, and inconsistencies in life. Through reflection and visionary meditation on dreams, you expand your understanding and experiential awareness to include the reality of nonordinary states of consciousness not bound by your personal ego. Such experiences profoundly change your life. They consistently teach you to recognize and realize that, on the other side of everything you believe to be the absolute truth, live contradictions that are also absolutely true.

Jung's personal experience with his dreams and with his patients'
dreams led him to an awareness that the ultimate result of self-reflection and dream work is the experience of the transpersonal dimension. This dimension has a sacred quality that appears in dreams as
the image or experience of numinous or creative energy. He describes
the psychic presence of the invisible spiritual archetype as demonstrating spontaneous movement and activity with the ability to produce and manipulate images independently of sense perception.[17] As
you continue soulful dream writing with collective transpersonal
material, your recognition and respect for what is beyond your personal ego grows stronger. When you write and develop these dreams,
you feel their numinous nature and become increasingly familiar with
the experience.

Transpersonal dreams contain spiritual archetypes in human, animal, and energetic forms that bring you counsel. They pull you into an
experience that is beyond the collective scope of myths and legends
into a direct experience of the numinous. I had the following dream,
which is an example of the animal archetype of the serpent. Over many
years, serpents have appeared as transpersonal characters in my dreams.

*I enter a classroom. I look around. The front of the room is to my left and directly
in front of me are rows of old-fashioned wooden school desks facing the front of the
room. A large, heavy wooden table is in the front of them. This is for the professor,
who is a woman. I am the teaching assistant in the class. I see about twelve students
in the room waiting for the instructor, who I know is out of town on a speaking
tour. I am to lead the class.*

*I am standing by a student's desk when the linoleum begins to crack in a line
from the front of the room toward me. I step up on a chair as an enormous serpent
rises up next to me. "She" is multicolored, a rainbow of magenta pink, brilliant yellow, and bright emerald stripes. She coils and rises up to the ceiling and turns her
head slowly as she surveys everyone in the class.*

The students are stunned. I watch the serpent, wondering what she will do. A telephone rings; it is the professor leaving a message saying she will not be back for the class and that I should take over. The serpent swivels her head toward me and looks me straight in the eyes. Then she sinks down, and retraces her path, flowing rapidly back in the direction of the professor's desk. She turns right and pushes open a door at the side of the desk and disappears. I follow her through the door and fall into open space. As I fall, I see the planets and the stars and I feel safe. I enjoy free falling.

The serpent is a potent archetypal symbol. It has been variously described as a symbol of how the individual heals the wounds of past experiences, and as a symbol of change and the birth of a new attitude. As such, it carries associations of tension and balance. My immediate personal response to it in this dream is that it's my literal-left-brain-vs.-my-mythic-right-brain conflict again! The serpent is leading me out of the box of the rational into the vastness of the unexplored realm of experience. Several years later, I became aware that this dream was prospective, because it foreshadowed a course of study in shamanic practice that has facilitated my ability to hold the tension of the opposites as I balance between the objectivity of concepts and the subjective depths of my experiences. As you learn through visionary meditation and dream writing to hold the tension that is inevitable when you experience opposition and contradiction, you move along the personal path to creative individuation. Your dreams present you with the perfect paradoxes you need to understand what is unfolding within your psyche. These discoveries help you gain insight through dreams so you can continue to explore the fringes of your capacity for awareness and creative expression and discover some new, third experience.

When you have a difficult time gaining insight into a dream, it is usually because it reflects some unrecognized aspect of your psyche. It may be a new awareness that is trying to become conscious and is reflected in the image of the dream. When the images come from your collective transpersonal psyche, they contain unfamiliar mysterious archetypal characters that are not yet a part of your awareness or experience. A dream with such a mysterious quality invites you to pay closer attention to what is going on in your unconscious, as well as in your personal life and the surrounding world.

Even when a dream intuitively feels as though it comes from your transpersonal psyche, try to relate its dream images to your outer life. Wonder how outer events are influencing you. Always try to explore your dreams on a subjective level first, as if each character and image is a symbol of an aspect of your individual psyche. If a character in a dream is well-known and currently an active part of your life, however, the dream may, in fact, be about that person.

The most useful way to look at all dreams is to include both the personal and the collective transpersonal perspectives. Once you have a personal sense of the dream, explore it at the collective and transpersonal levels. Although a particular dream may lean in one direction or another, most numinous and emotionally charged dreams contain kernels of wisdom from both the personal and the transpersonal realms.

When you are learning the language of your dreams, you may find a dream mentor helpful. An objective, qualified professional can help you discover the symbolic language of your dreams. And you can learn a great deal about your dreams through dream writing and journaling. Your dreams are your private stories. They are gifts. Their purpose is to guide you in your personal, creative, and spiritual development. Since the most important information about your dreams comes from your own experience and associations, go ahead and speculate about their meaning. If you are wrong, future dreams, visionary meditations, and writings will clarify your speculations.

6

visionary
meditation
and writing

*Active imagination [visionary meditation], as the term denotes,
means that the images have a life of their own and that the symbolic events develop
according to their own logic—that is, of course, if your conscious reason
does not interfere. You begin by concentrating upon a starting point.*

—C. G. JUNG, *CW* 18, ¶ 397

Visionary meditation writing differs from journaling in that it is a method of using images, chance associations, and spontaneous fantasies that arise during a period of active imagination to expand and explore dreams without deliberately directing what unfolds. This type of meditation, in which you guide and focus your mind so you can interact with your dreams through writing, encourages a dream to progress without intentionally deviating from the thrust of the dream. I have borrowed the term "visionary meditation" from Jung to describe the second phase of this dream-writing practice. It fits with my intention to emphasize the meditative aspect of this approach and more accurately describes my experience of the process. Like Jung, I liken the role of the dreaming soul to that of an inner guru.[1] The dreaming soul is the wise entity, the inner guru, that communicates with you through the metaphors of your dreams and makes your visionary meditation a sacred experience that you revere and respect.

Jung developed the practice of using visionary meditation with dreams because he realized that, if we interpret dreams too literally, we tend to miss their symbolic significance. If you reduce the images and themes of your dreams to their literal meaning, such as those found in many dream interpretation books, you tend to miss the unique value of the dream metaphor. If you use prescribed interpretations, you tend to reduce the creative quality of the dream to dull banality. As James Hollis observes, "Without the tools of metaphor and symbol we would have precious little to say, for they allow us to talk about that about which we cannot talk."[2] It is worthwhile, however, to consult a variety of sources for hints about the possible significance of your dreams. The process of understanding a dream involves psychological empathy, intuition, and knowledge of the world. It is important to get around using stereotypical interpretations and to approach each new dream with curiosity and an appreciation for the unexpected.

When you first observe a dream, you participate in what Jungian analyst Barbara Hannah calls a "passive imagination process [that] is ... like watching a cinema."[3] When you hold the dream in your awareness and shift into a state of visionary meditation, you can access spontaneous associations that allow the mood and images of the dream to continue. Try the mindfulness breathing meditation in Exercise 13 to help you shift into a state of visionary meditation.

Exercise 13:
Mindfulness Breathing for Visionary Meditation

Focus your intention on relaxing and meditating to turn your attention inward. Close your eyes and take a minute or so to relax your body. Mentally focus on your body and relax each muscle group, from the top of your head to the tips of your fingers and the tips of your toes. Then bring your attention to your breath. Don't do anything about your breathing; just notice where and how you feel the sensations of your breath in your body. Where do you feel the sensation of your breath in your body? As you inhale, notice that sensation in your nostrils and then follow the feeling down into your chest. Where do you feel your breath in your body when you come to the end of the inhalation?

Then track your breath as you begin to exhale. Pay attention to the sensation in your body that accompanies every nanosecond of the path of your exhalation. What do you feel in your chest, your belly, your legs and feet, your arms, shoulders, neck and head? This focus on the micro-progress of your breath as you inhale and exhale, as the cycles of your breath develop a deep and rhythmic pattern, is the core of mindfulness breathing. As you follow your breath, notice your thoughts. Each time you notice a thought, bring your attention back to your breath. Where do you feel your breath in your body? Reconnect with your breath at that point and follow the sensation throughout the rest of that breath cycle, and the next, and the next. Each time your mind wanders to a random thought or image, bring it back to your breath. When your breath pattern has deepened and you can feel the breath in and out of your belly, picture the image or situation from the dream on which you are focused. Stay with that and let whatever happens happen. As the dream continues in the theater of your mind, you are in the state of visionary meditation. Exercise 14 will help you choose and work with various aspects of a dream.

Once again, as with the original dream material, put words around images, ideas, and intuitive associations that come up in your visionary meditation. Remember, this form of writing is not journaling. Instead of making personal associations or interpretations, you are the scribe recording what you noticed in the meditation. This writing is exactly like writing the original dream. Use the first-person present-tense fast-narrative style as you put words around your meditation experience.

◆   ◆   ◆

Writing without contrivance takes practice. When I first began, my efforts were strained and overly fictionalized as I tried to elaborate my dream stories. In time, I was able to sense when I was trying too hard to make something happen. Once I learned to let the story unfold by itself, I was amazed and excited by the way the process further informed my dreams, stimulated my conscious imagination, and enriched my expressive and creative writing.

Your ability to write with comfort from the flow of what emerges grows stronger as you move back and forth between imaginative, symbolic, and metaphoric images and literal thinking. As you learn to recognize the difference between spontaneous visions and images, and more literal ideas and images, you also learn to blend both sources of inspiration. Try the following writing exercise to practice writing a verbal sketch in visionary meditation based on a dream. Choose a dream that is alive for you, one you are curious about and that has caught your attention.

Exercise 14:
A Verbal Sketch in Visionary Meditation

Focus your intention on relaxing and meditating to turn your attention inward. Close your eyes and begin mindfulness breathing as you turn your attention inward. Start with a point of interest from the dream, close your eyes, and focus on that image or sensation. Let yourself go into a reverie of visionary meditation with the intention of "seeing" the dream develop and progress. Meditate on your memories and mental images of the dream until you imaginatively reenter the experience of the dream and new images begin to flow. Follow the flow of what spontaneously emerges and stay with that flow of images.

Continue with your eyes closed until the flow of images is strong enough to hold them in your mind's eye, along with the sequence of events or a character's actions, as you open your literal eyes and write a verbal sketch narrating your inner vision. Keep your pen on the paper—or your fingers on the keys, or your voice inscribing a tape—and let the story flow. Practice shifting back and forth between the spontaneous images and ideas that come to you and release any conscious efforts to contrive a story while you continue writing. As you write, allow your imaginative fantasy to develop on its own as you gently add your awareness of your emotional and physical responses to the dream into the original dream material.

◆ ◆ ◆

Jung believed that visionary meditation is a way of forming a link with the creative potential of the unconscious psyche. Dream writing will help you to access and become conscious of positive and negative complexes or systems of energy that influence your thoughts, feelings, and behaviors. Visionary meditation writing will help you re-collect the energy from a self-limiting complex and redirect it into creative writing.

A complex is a conglomeration of energy that originates when you have an intense response to a powerful positive or negative emotional experience. Every subsequent experience that feels similar attaches itself like a magnet to the nucleus of that original experience. Imagine how powerful a complex can become. Over time, if comparable experiences continue, a more complicated body of emotional force grows into a larger and more autonomous system of associations.

For example, a penchant for music can be a positive complex of harmonic energy or it can be a negative complex of cacophonic energy. A predilection for humor can be a positive complex of joy or a negative complex of conceit. A tendency toward seriousness can be a positive complex of earnestness or a negative complex of moroseness. A complex of energy that is encouraged over time can grow into an autonomous power that can positively or negatively impact your thoughts, feelings, and behaviors. What is really important about such complexes of energy is that you may not be aware of their influence. It is precisely because they have such a powerful effect on you, however, that it is important for your personal growth that you become mindful of their influences. This is possible when you attend to your dreams, because your dreams present your complexes to you through their symbols and metaphors.

Is it necessary to become conscious of your complexes to express yourself creatively? One of the reasons I began to follow my dreams was to learn about my complexes, because I sensed that my dreams were the origin of whatever creative potential I had. Although I had kept a written record of my dreams for years, I didn't do much with them until I developed this dream-writing practice. I was caught up in left-brain, linear concepts. I was animus possessed. Then about a decade ago I had a dream. I sat straight up in bed and shouted, "I get the concept; I just don't get the experience!" I literally woke myself up. I was so affected by the voice in this dream message that I was compelled to delve even deeper into my dreams. I *knew*; I "got" the experience that tending more closely to the metaphors of my dreams would lead me into the depths of my psyche. That would be the path to the inner experience for me. One of the values of visionary meditation is that it offers you the opportunity to explore a dimension of nonrational experience that is available to you through your dreams. When you expand dreams that portray constellations of emotional energy so they can be assimilated, the energy that you reclaim becomes available for other experiences. As Jung explains, "The energy becomes serviceable again by being brought into play through man's conscious attitude towards the collective [transpersonal] unconscious."[4] Focusing your attention inward, in a process of visionary meditation, leads to what Jung describes as a form of communion with your higher Self.

DIRECTING YOUR SECOND ATTENTION

The second attention is a way of perceiving the experience you have during visionary meditation. This nonordinary mode of perception is similar to a lucid dreaming experience in which you become aware of participating in a dream at the time it is taking place. You access the power of your mind to form images and participate in nonlinear reality. The act of observing and participating in the dream affects it in some non-intentional, organic way that becomes part of the evolving dream.

The actual felt sense of the second attention is like the experience of becoming aware that you are dreaming while you are dreaming. Don Juan explains the second attention in a way that is applicable to dream writing, and prose and poetry writing:

> As a preamble to his first lesson in dreaming, don Juan talked about the second attention as a progression: beginning as an idea that comes to us more like a curiosity than an actual possibility; turning into something that can only be felt, as a sensation is felt; and finally evolving into a state of being, or realm of practicalities, or a preeminent force that opens for us worlds beyond our wildest fantasies.[5]

Don Juan used different terms, but essentially he taught Carlos to use the art of dreaming to see into and experience what Jung referred to as the "little hidden door in the innermost and most secret recesses of the soul."[6] Don Juan taught Carlos to remember his dreams, to participate intentionally in them, and eventually to travel to other worlds through shamanic dreaming. "'Dreams are, if not a door, a hatch into other worlds,' he began. 'As such, dreams are a two-way street. Our awareness goes through that hatch into other realms, and those other realms send scouts into our dreams.'"[7]

From Jung's psychological point of view, the realms of those other worlds are within the unconscious psyche. Others such as Christ, Buddha, and various shamanic teachers, took a metaphysical point of view and suggested that the realms of the unconscious may connect the psyche to the web of universal energy that connects everyone and everything. Such metaphysical systems are based on extremely abstract reasoning that is considered by Western scientific thinking to be highly theoretical and speculative.

The term "metaphysical" is associated with experiences that lack a material body, substance, or form and, therefore, it is often used to refer to transpersonal and numinous spiritual experiences. Although Jung objected to being called a metaphysician, he did not reject the realm of metaphysics. He said there is no doubt that numinous experiences that may be divine interventions do occur, but, at least during his time, this realm was not subject to irrefutable scientific proof. Jung was devoted to grounding metaphysical experience within the human psyche. He had no quarrel with the fact that numinous phenomena exist within the human psyche. Nor would he quarrel with the idea that mystical experiences are projections of the individuation process that are felt to be outside of the human psyche. The metaphysician would merely add that the projection goes both ways. God is projecting you at the same time that you are projecting God. Like the shaman and metaphysician, if you are open to the visions of your transpersonal psyche, you may have numinous experiences. In many cultures, the shaman, like don Juan, acts as a medium who enters an ecstatic dream state between the visible world and the invisible spirit world to retrieve lost soul parts and unconscious possibilities for healing. Dream writing promotes a personal and transpersonal awareness that can be similar to shamanic soul retrieval dreaming. When you dream, you may also experience ecstatic journeys beyond your personal psyche. By retrieving them and uniting them with your conscious psyche, you can heal and develop your own ecstatic creativity.

Dream-writing practice can help you strengthen your numinous night wings so you can travel to realms of experience available within and perhaps beyond your psyche. Such experiences teach you to recognize and expand your nonliteral modes of perception. You are at home with symbol and metaphor. You can see beyond the dimension of logic into the many possibilities of your imagination. In this state, you discover what is possible, even if it seems improbable. Dr. Villoldo's mentor tells him, "We can think, my friend. We can dream with our eyes open. We can travel throughout the universe, free from time and space and the need to understand. . . . It is our imagination that must be allowed to evolve, set free, nourished, nurtured, because . . . with imagination we can hold a universe inside our minds."[8] Villoldo speaks to the evolution of our imagination.

THE WAY OF UNDERSTANDING

There are two ways to focus on dream material during visionary meditation. One is the way of understanding, on which we will focus in this chapter; the other is the way of creative formulation, which we will explore in chapter 7. The primary intentions in personal dream writing are to understand the purpose and sense the meaning of dreams for personal growth. The objective is to extend the dream material through visionary meditation to provide a dynamic context to consciously experience the vital intention of a dream.

When you write the first draft of an original dream story with the intention of understanding the meaning of the metaphor, there is no need to concern yourself with the aesthetics or style of your writing. Once you have the original dream in writing, let yourself wonder about and intuit the significance and purpose of the dream. Don't come to any conclusions. As you write the narrative of the dream, hold the mental images and turn them around in your imagination to observe the patterns within them. Later, as the mystery continues in visionary meditation and you write what you see, add your associations and amplifications in parenthesis as you elaborate the dream material.

When you track your dreams for understanding, tune in to your emotional dream body. Wonder and journal about how those emotions are relevant to some aspect of your current life situation. At the physical level, emotions are biochemical molecules that change in response to events and the meaning you give to those events. For example, an experience that initially elicits fear may change to one that prompts anger once you decide you are safe enough to react assertively or aggressively. The emotions and moods you experience in dreams are a result of the dynamic tension that exists between your conscious and your unconscious experiences. This vigorous tension activates your dreaming body and biochemically creates an emotion that sets the tone for the meaning of a dream story. You feel all combinations of joy, anger, fear, or sadness as intensely in your dreams as you do in waking life. In fact, some emotions may be more intense in your dreams than they are when you are awake, because you do not have the same ability to avoid them when you are sleeping.

When you remember and write a dream, you can feel those emotions again. The dream is asking you to look for the presence or absence of those emotions in your life. An erotic dream that excites you asks you to explore the presence or absence of passion in your life. A joyful dream asks you to contemplate the presence or absence of experiences of delight and appreciation. Dreams of loss leave an ache in your emotional body that suggests the presence of unresolved sadness and grief. A dream of tender love surrounds you with a warm contented embrace. How are you embracing your life, or not? How are you being embraced? A sluggish and heavy dream encourages you to look for ways you are stuck or oppressed. A fearful dream reflects apprehension about something in your life experience. Anger in a dream reflects anger in your life.

One way to flesh out a dream story in order to understand how it relates to your life is to focus on the emotional sensations you feel in your body as you experience and then remember the dream. Concentrate on how and where you experience sensations in your body; try to name the emotions at the same time. Often, you can regain a dream that is drifting away by tuning in to your emotional body sensations and reentering the dream through those sensations.

The four core emotions of fear, sadness, anger, and joy are often felt in relatively specific areas of the body. Fear tends to be felt in the belly, sadness in the chest, and anger in the head. They are survival emotions and predominate because survival is a prime directive of life. These emotions motivate you to respond to intrusion, warn you of danger, and help you experience loss. The fourth core emotion, joy, is a diffuse sensation of pleasure that you may experience in a particular area of your body or throughout your entire body. Joy is that "incredible lightness of being" that can be peaceful or could be ecstatic. Joy can transport you into a spiritual relationship with what is sacred for you. Your dreams use combinations or variations of these emotions to encourage you to pay attention to the ways in which they are active in your current life situations. As you feel the experiences in your body, as well as in your memory, you are moved sensually and emotionally. To be touched by a dream in this way draws you into the core of your emotional imagination. When you remember and put words around your emotional dream-body experiences in the state of visionary meditation, you can generate a flow of images and ideas that help you move the dream story forward. This process helps you move your life story forward as well by stimulating your curiosity and imagination.

The breathing practice in Exercise 15 is a way to literally touch the soulful energy of your emotional body. Try to experience and activate the emotional sensations in your body, as an actor calls forth an emotional response of a character. Practice this exercise to become familiar with a variety of emotional sensations. They include combinations and extensions of the core emotions of anger, fear, sadness, and joy. Let yourself touch and express your emotions. Laugh if you feel like laughing. Cry if you feel like crying. Be angry if that is your emotion. If you are afraid, feel the fear and journal about your fear.

Exercise 15:
Contacting Your Emotional Body

This exercise will take about ten minutes. You will be using the abdominal breathing method you learned in Exercise 1. The purpose of this exercise is to feel in your body the sensations that accompany your emotions. Practice this exercise every morning, or as early as possible. At first, do the exercise for only ten minutes. Once you are familiar with how it feels, you can practice for as long as you like.

Begin by lying down on your back on a firm, comfortable surface. An exercise mat works well. Straighten your spine; rest your arms along the sides of your body. Bend your knees and place your feet flat on the surface a comfortable width apart to support your legs. Focus your intention on relaxing and meditating to turn your attention inward. Close your eyes and begin abdominal breathing. As you breathe in through your nose, follow the sensation of your breath as you fully expand your abdomen. As you exhale, fully release and relax your abdomen. When you are breathing rhythmically, begin to gently arch your back as you inhale. Arch your spine only slightly; do not strain. When you have come to the end of the inhalation and your abdomen is fully extended and your spine is slightly arched, begin to exhale and allow your spine to descend and flatten along the surface. When you complete your exhalation, your spine is flat and your muscles are relaxed. Rest for a few seconds and repeat this for a couple of minutes. Then rest again for a minute. Notice the sensations in your belly, chest, and head.

Next, allow your spine to remain relaxed and flat as you inhale, expand your abdomen fully, hold your breath, and, as you hold, tighten and release your belly very sharply and very quickly. You should feel a movement up into your diaphragm and chest. Do this as many times as you can without straining. Then exhale and relax for about ten seconds. Repeat the quick tightening and releasing of your belly for a couple of minutes. Then rest again for a minute. Notice the sensations in your belly, chest, and head.

Finally, while remaining relaxed, make sure your spine is straight, your knees bent, and your feet firmly on the floor. Extend your arms straight out, perpendicular to your body. Keeping your shoulders down, allow your knees to fall gently to the right while you roll your head to the left. Now move your knees to the left while you roll your head to the right.

Feel the gentle stretch of your spine. Now inhale as you move your head to one side, and exhale as you move it to the other. Do this slowly and gently for a couple of minutes. Then straighten your legs and rest, breathing naturally for a couple of minutes. As you rest, notice the sensations in your belly, chest, head, and entire body. Make notes in your journal about what you feel and try to describe the sensations in the areas of your body associated with the four core emotions—fear in the belly, sadness in the chest, anger in the head, and joy throughout your body.

◆ ◆ ◆

When you connect with your emotional body through your breath, let go and drop into visionary meditation and shift from focusing on a concrete literal idea to opening yourself to the flow of imaginative fantasy. The "drop" happens when you choose to let go of your focus on the outside world and instead focus on the inner world of images and sensations that emerge as you contemplate the original dream. Your emotional energy is the core of the dream material that inspires and expands your dream into new possibilities. Try the following exercise for another way to access your emotional dream body during visionary meditation.

Exercise 16:
Contacting Your Emotional Dream Body

To activate your emotional energy body during visionary meditation, choose a dream you experienced emotionally. Read it, then focus your intention on relaxing and meditating to turn your attention inward. Close your eyes and take about ten minutes to be with the memory of the dream as you practice the first part of the breathing exercises for contacting your emotional body.

You may lie down or do the exercise in a chair. With your eyes still closed, inhale slowly, arch your back, and expand your abdomen. Then exhale and relax your abdomen, allowing your back to relax. Repeat this pattern as you center and meditate on the mental image of the dream while you breathe, until you imaginatively reenter the memory experience of the dream. Feel yourself drop down into your emotional dream body as you remember and experience the emotions, images, and events of the dream. Feel your self shift into visionary meditation where new images emerge. Continue breathing at a comfortable pace. It is no longer necessary to arch and relax your back, unless you feel like doing so.

As you continue to remember the dream, allow your witnessing ego to observe, but not interfere with, the memory. Continue to maintain contact with the dream state by sensing and re-engaging the emotional experience you had in your body during the dream or as you awoke from the dream. Notice where you feel the sensation of emotion in your body. In your head (anger, frustration, or peace), your chest (sadness, hurt, or wholeness), your belly (fear, anxiety, or unity)?

Concentrate on your emotional state and notice the transformations and spontaneous fantasies that develop. Stay in touch with the feeling of the emotional aliveness you feel and write from that aliveness. Let whatever emotions, images, characters, situations, or settings you notice emerge without censoring or editing. Keep your pen on the paper and keep writing until the feeling and the images fade and stop.

♦ ♦ ♦

When you finish writing in this context, you may want to journal about how the feelings you experienced are relevant to your current life situation. As you reconnect with the emotional sensations of your dream, its vital intention becomes more understandable. You realize that the dream is more than a fantasy, more than a random firing of brain cells that causes pictures to appear in your mind's eye while you sleep. You discover what the dream is teaching your imaginative and your rational self. As you put words around the emotions you feel on the inner stage of your dreams, you also discover how to integrate your emotional truth in your life as you express yourself on its outer stage.

What is not managed on the outer stage of life will appear in a dream. When such dreams are not attended to and given an outer form, they are repressed, ignored, or not applied to life. So they repeat themselves in future dreams and in emotional or physical disturbance in your outer life. These "real-life" experiences reflect the message of your dream. What is not integrated on the inner stage of your psyche will inevitably occur on the outer stage of your life and force a confrontation with the need for change. This cycle of inner and outer dramatic conflict will continue until you pay attention to the signals and take responsibility for changing the dynamics that you repeat and repeat and repeat.

An unresolved conflict may show itself in physical symptoms such as fatigue, headache, muscle tension, or irritable bowel. It may show itself in emotional symptoms such as irritability, anxiety, depression, or poor concentration. The conflict may appear as difficulty at work or in personal relationships. The continuation of conflict in your outer life will be reflected in the inner world of your dreams as the emotional energy that is energized by your outer-life situation. Thus, an interactive and related cycle of inner and outer experiences seeks to encourage you toward change and growth.

Here's an example of this interaction. A married woman, Elizabeth, was having an affair with a married man, Frank. She told her husband, William, and for personal reasons, he did not object. Frank chose not to tell his wife, Ellen. Elizabeth was uncomfortable, but rationalized that the issue was between Frank and Ellen.

During the affair, Elizabeth had several dreams that Frank was unfaithful to her with yet another woman. She also had several dreams in which she was in a bed in a secret room inside Frank and Ellen's home. Frank could enter the room from inside his house, but Elizabeth could only enter and leave through a separate, disguised exit. She had several dreams, with several different story lines, in which she was in Frank's house when his wife and/or other members of his family were present. In all of those dreams, Elizabeth was invisible. She could see and hear them, but they could not see or hear her.

She had other dreams in which she was inside her house with Frank and they were both invisible to her husband. The dreams concerned her, so she talked to Frank about them. He denied that he was involved with anyone else and soothed her concerns about the secret room. He suggested the dreams were reflecting how much she loved him and he was honored. So Elizabeth ignored the dreams, choosing to believe they were just anxiety dreams.

One day, Frank wrote Elizabeth a poetic and passionate note. After he read it to her on the phone, he accidentally left the notebook on the table next to his chair. Ellen innocently looked through the notebook and read the note. She was hurt and angry, and confronted them both. They all agreed that the affair would cease.

The lovers tried to stop their affair, but gave in to the pleasures of the moment. Elizabeth rationalized once again that the issue of dishonesty was between Frank and his wife. When the dreams about being in her lover's home and being invisible returned, she began to sense they were warning her. She continued the affair for a while, but she could not completely ignore the dreams. Her passion began to fade and she gradually began to distance herself from Frank. She strove for almost a year to resolve her ambivalence and continued to distance herself emotionally and physically from him.

One day, Frank accidentally left his email open and Ellen innocently read a passionate note he had written to Elizabeth. Ellen was again enraged and demanded that Frank and Elizabeth never have contact with each other again. In fact, she demanded that they be invisible to each other. Although Elizabeth was upset by the second accidental betrayal, she was also relieved that a resolution was being forced on her lover. She accepted responsibility for her part in the betrayal and realized that, if she had attended to and understood what was happening on the inner stage of her dreams, she might have resolved her own ambivalence sooner and prevented a lot of emotional suffering for everyone. The next time Frank suggested they get together, she found it less difficult to say no.

Ignorance is not bliss; it is denial. When you ignore certain dreams, an event on the outer stage of your life is likely to force you into a confrontation with something you have denied and kept unconscious. This is what Jung means when he refers to a one-sided conscious position. When you consciously or unconsciously avoid seeing what contradicts your opinions and beliefs, you are practicing denial.

Dream-writing practice is one way to stop participating in denial and arrive at a position of clarity and truth. To do so, you must be willing to let go of certain illusions that have served you. To willingly let go means to discover your authentic truth. That level of freedom from mistaken perceptions of reality frees you from the unconscious tyrants that otherwise feed your illusions and make your life a soap-opera drama.

Of course, outer situations can be settled without consulting dreams. However, dreams can help you find resolutions. Working with dreams is a process of enrichment. Expanding them through visionary meditation brings them closer to consciousness and thus instigates change and the possibility of something new. When you collaborate with your dreaming soul, you contact "entities which exert an attractive force upon the conscious mind."[9] Sometimes these entities are complimentary; sometimes they are critical.

During the process of visionary meditation, spontaneous and uncontrived images and themes unfold. Allow these images to develop voluntarily and put words around them. Writing these spontaneous images, scenes, plots, and dialogues based on dreams helps you discover what you can create from your dream material. Exercise 17 will help you write these images in a productive way.

Exercise 17:
Writing Your Visionary Meditations

Choose a dream and read your first draft. Focus your intention on relaxing and meditating to turn your attention inward. Concentrate on reliving the memory and emotional experience of the dream just before you close your eyes and begin visionary meditation. This sets the stage to continue the dream by reviewing it with the intention of experiencing it as fully as possible while awake. Barbara Hannah suggests that "the first step in active imagination is to learn . . . to see or hear the dream while awake."[10] Do this by tending to the dream image until something begins to change.

Observe what develops as objectively as possible, while writing everything you notice in fast-narrative form. This way of writing helps you discover meaningful themes in your psyche. It is also a good way to keep yourself engaged in writing. In time, many of the symbols that your passive imagination sends you in dream stories will become familiar to you. They are the kernels of insight that inform your writing and mature into stories, poems, and other forms of writing.

◆ ◆ ◆

You can transform and create the story you are now living when you pay attention to the relationship between the dramas of your inner and outer life. When you reflect on your life and your dreams, you become empowered to live more consciously. My father often reminded me of the words of Socrates: "The unexamined life is not worth living." While that may not be true for everyone, it is true for anyone who wants to heal and develop creative potential.

It takes courage to fly into your unconscious psyche and relate to the awesome power of your dreaming soul. You meet that aspect of your Self that informs you as the author, writer, director, and producer of your dream stories. Your dreams lead you to discover that the tragic, romantic, or comic plots that take place in your dreams are often reflected in your personal life and vice versa. You also meet that aspect of your shadow self that is your inner critic. To develop your creative writing potential, you must face both your inner and outer critics.

WRITING AND YOUR INNER CRITIC

When you write, you at times come face to face with your inner critic. So let's deal with that critic now. In this writing practice, there are no rules about grammar or punctuation or the criteria of formal writing. Once you write the first draft of a dream, there are no rules requiring you to stay with the facts of the dream or limit writing to the facts of your life. You write to invent possibilities. You write to analyze, criticize, and reinvent your life. You write to heal yourself. You write to express your life experiences. You write for fun. And you write because you cannot not write. You write to resolve issues, and one of those issues may be self-criticism.

The voice of your inner critic requires and deserves attention. So give it a separate journal to write in and fully express its criticism.[11] Let your critic have its say in a sort of parallel reality with the creative writer in you, so it has a forum to express itself. If you discover you have several different types of critics, try giving each of them a separate journal. As your separate notebooks fill with valuable material, you will sharpen your writing skills. Be open to challenges from your inner critic. Be open to the possibility that, beneath the harsh words, there may be some genuine wisdom in what your critic has to say. You may discover that your critic is not always your enemy.

At a certain point in the writing process, your critic can help you develop your writing craft. The challenge is to form a positive alliance and promote your critic to a supportive editor who can help develop congruence between your thoughts and feelings, and your writing process. Exercise 18 can help you develop this skill.

Exercise 18:
Your Inner Critic

When your ego is in a controlling or critical mood, trying too hard to make something happen and being critical of what you are writing, give it a separate place to write. Give it its own journal. Give your ego permission to try as hard as it likes and to criticize what you are writing or experiencing as much as it wants. Let all the thoughts and feelings spill out on the pages of your critical ego's personal journal. Allow those thoughts and criticisms to keep spilling and spilling, until a bit of clarity begins to emerge. That clarity will feel as if a veil has lifted between your ego's hunger to be a writer and your authentic desire to write.

Your critic will not cease to attack you if you are defensive or feel defeated. It is not necessary to agree or disagree with it. Trying to reason with it can turn into a never-ending debate. Instead, acknowledge your critic's right to an opinion and, when the opinion is fully expressed, get back to your writing. Give your critical ego's journal a title like, Wisdom from My Inner Critic. Then return to the visionary meditation you are writing.

◆ ◆ ◆

The intention during visionary meditation writing is to let whatever flows out of your passive imagination rise into awareness in written form. The written visionary meditation below demonstrates the increase in understanding and assimilation of an experience that is a result of dream-writing practice. It also illustrates how dream writing becomes story telling. If you reread my Storm Troopers dream (see page 29), and then read the visionary meditation below, you will notice how the characters, plot, emotional tone, and actions in the visionary meditation flow out of the original dream. The vignette reaches a conclusion that is relevant to my personal experience as the dreamer. The experience of coming to a conclusion marks the end of a visionary-meditation writing session. Usually, this is the end of the personal aspect of dream-writing practice, which is to explore and assimilate the meaning of your dreams.

As I stand at the southwest corner of a field of death the size of a city block, I stare in horror at the rows and rows of dead children's bodies laid out before me. There must be hundreds of them. The book I am holding contains colored photographs of all the children arranged in rows just like the bodies are arranged in rows on the ground in front of me. The book and my heart are heavy as I hold it open, like a bible, in my two hands. I look down at the pictures and then out across the field.

So many children! One three-year-old boy wears a red ski hat and holds a Mickey Mouse doll in his lifeless arms. My chest is heavy and tight. I force myself to breathe against the pressure of my diaphragm. I squeeze the muscles of my throat as tightly as I can. I must capture my scream before it erupts and invites the gun shot to my head.

A different row of parents are walking slowly toward me now. They are tiny people. Most of them come as couples, but some come alone. They have been told to come to me and I will help them find their children. I see the weeping parents as though I were far away, hovering in the sky above. I watch their procession of grief as they wind their way toward me between the dark fields of death.

I can see my own small self standing, holding the book, waiting. I sense my inner child trembling; she wants to drop the book and run screaming into that snaking onward stream of stunned and emotionally battered people. From above, I reach out my hand. She sighs as I touch her forehead and we join to finish our duty. I straighten my shoulders, stand tall, and meet the eyes of the first pair of parents. I turn the book of photos around and hold it out for them to study. "When you find your child in this book, touch the picture and I will show you where you can find your child in the field."

The father looks deeply into my eyes as if searching for the vision of some more tolerable reality. Finally, he looks down, studies the pages, and then touches the picture of his daughter. His tears fall on the picture as I turn to my left. "Over there, do you see her? She is next to the boy with the Mickey Mouse doll." The mother crumples beside him and he reaches down and lifts her to his side. He steadies her, encircling her shoulders gently, as he leads her down the row toward their child's body.

I look up into the eyes of the next parent, a strong woman, alone and waiting to gather her lost child in her arms. I steel myself to accept and carry out the challenge to my soul. I must remain calm and strong in order to help those who have lost their children claim and accept their losses.

This visionary meditation story illustrates how I continued to work with my extraordinarily telepathic dream. The process of writing helped me assimilate the reality of the fact that I actually had a telepathic dream, that it foreshadowed the actual death of my future son-in-law, and that it foreshadowed the fact that I was the only person who could notify his parents. I continued to work with visionary meditation and prose and poetry to assimilate additional dreams about this experience. I gave form to my shock and grief and my extrasensory experience in a way that helped me to assimilate the pain his death brought to my life and my family. My reading of Jung reassured me that such experiences are not unique and therefore I could trust my experience as real and valuable.

Try the next exercise to develop your skill with visionary-meditation writing and in writing a dream forward. Writing a dream forward in visionary meditation is like circling around it, observing it, and carefully stretching and sketching it with words to draw the energy out of the dream and into its potential form.

Exercise 19:
Writing a Dream Forward

Choose a dream you remember vividly. Focus your intention on relaxing and meditating to turn your attention inward. Begin mindfulness breathing and, when you are ready, meditate on the memory of the dream until you drop down into the dream experience and shift into creative visionary meditation.

Focus on whatever attracts your attention, stirs your imagination, and has energy for you. Choose a feeling, an image, a character, or whatever catches your attention and that you feel you want to develop. Imagine you are the element that has appeal for you. Empathize with that element. Allow images to flow through you from your creative unconscious into the stream of your conscious awareness.

As you write what flows from that stream of consciousness, without censoring anything, get in touch with a sense of the interplay between your dreaming soul and your aware ego. Allow yourself to write what emerges as long as the energy for writing continues.

When you feel the energy fade, stop writing. Take a break. You may break for ten minutes or an hour, for days or even weeks, until you feel the urge to review what you have written. Repeat the process and continue until the visionary meditation feels finished.

◆ ◆ ◆

The next exercise can help you write forward a dream that seems to be related to your personal life.

Exercise 20:
Visionary Meditation on a Personal Dream

Choose a dream that seems to reflect your personal life. Read it and focus on the story and characters. Choose an aspect you want to start with and focus your intention on relaxing and meditating to turn your attention inward. Begin mindfulness breathing meditation. When you are ready, focus on the mental image until you imaginatively reenter the memory experience of the dream. Feel yourself shift into visionary meditation. Keep your focus on the memory experience of the dream and observe how the story begins to unfold or change.

Tune into the emotional sensations of the dream and let spontaneous associations alter and develop the dream story. Stay with the emotional experience of the dream and allow yourself to feel your emotions as vividly as possible. Allow what you feel to take the lead as you write. Do not censor anything that emerges. As you write, notice and experience your emotions. Let them inform your writing until you feel you are finished.

◆ ◆ ◆

You can use your dream-writing practice as a loom to weave a tapestry of your dreams, throughout your life and into the future. As you write the stories of your dreams, day after day, year after year, decade after decade, the patterns of your soul are revealed. This is the way to shed light on the deeper purposes of a dream. "A dream belongs in a series," Jung tells us. "Since there is continuity of consciousness, despite the fact that it is regularly interrupted by sleep, there is probably also a continuity of the unconscious processes—perhaps even more than with the events of consciousness."[12] Exercise 21 can help you develop a dream tapestry.

Exercise 21:
Weaving a Dream Tapestry

Read through your dreams once a week, once a month, and once a year to step back from the weaving process and see the pattern of your life unfolding. Keep an ongoing, dated, single-sentence synopsis of the main image or theme of each dream so you can find a dream later when you want to refer to it again. As you weave them together, and contemplate what you have woven, you discover the archetypes at work in your psyche.

◆　◆　◆

As you practice dream writing, you learn to translate and expand the language and symbolic metaphors of your dreams. This kind of writing is a powerful tool for coming into relationship with your dreams and thus your own inner wisdom. This practice also strengthens your writing skills and may become the springboard for other writing, such as personal essays, stories, or poems.

As you explore the ways in which your passive imagination presents a dream that follows the elements of dramatic structure you find in novels, poetry, and other forms of creative writing, you recognize the dramatic structure of your dreams. Then you can use it intentionally to lead your dreams into prose, poetry, and story writing.

7

intentional imagination and creative writing

What the poet beholds . . . is in truth the "Spirit" as ever it was, namely the totality of primary forms from which the archetypal images come. In this world of the collective [transpersonal] unconscious spirit appears as an archetype which is endowed with supreme significance and is expressed through the figure of the divine hero.

—C. G. JUNG, *CW* 5, ¶ 641

Visionary meditation writing is done with the intention of "switching off consciousness, at least to a relative extent, thus giving the unconscious contents a chance to develop."[1] You shift from receiving the material uncensored from your passive imagination to allowing the dream material to elaborate itself. This type of writing helps you understand your dreams and access the power of your mind to form images and put words around them. Then you can use what flows as a springboard for intentional imagination and creative writing.

Intentional writing may be inspired by the structure and story line of the original dream and/or the visionary meditation, but it expands that material further by adding a more deliberate component in which you, as the writer, play an increasingly active and deliberate part. In addition to the chance associations and spontaneous fantasies you elaborated in visionary meditation writing, you now apply some of the principles of dramatic structure to intentionally extending your story. One way to begin this process is to focus on any image that stands out for you and catches your interest, then follow the threads of new ideas and their associations.

POETRY AND PROSE

The language of your dreams transforms as you expand and express the inspiration they offer through poetry and prose. You can use prose, the language of ordinary speech and writing, to articulate concepts of reason and logical, rational, analytical thought. When you write in this way, you use a more clear-cut structure—the straightforward, direct, candid, and matter-of-fact language of formal essays and literature. The sequence of sounds and rhythm in prose is not as formal as in poetry. However, when you infuse such writing with a lyrical quality, your prose may approach poetic expressiveness.

Poetry, with its more formal rhythms, is the language you use to give expression to your emotional experiences. Your poetry may have an intentional rhythm expressed through a formal pattern of stressed and unstressed elements or syllables, or it may have the natural rhythm of free verse. You can combine poetry and prose to provide an infusion of emotion that brings your conceptual writing to life. Like melodic music, poetry has a harmonic sound that is pleasing to the ear. Many pieces of prose have a poetic rhythm and some poems, like those of Shakespeare, tell a story in dramatic form. Some dreams have a melodic, orchestrated quality that flows into poetic prose.

Every time you write a dream story with the intention of crafting it to blend and extend the literal and emotional experience of the dream, you strengthen your writing style and deepen your writing voice. There are dreams that are entire dramatic plots with fully fleshed-out protagonists, antagonists, dialogues, and settings. Such dreams tell a story that is compelling on its own. Some entice you to flesh out the hint of a story waiting to unfold. Often, the flow of images, ideas, characters, and plot progresses toward a resolution.

Writing your dreams into prose and poetry is a way to increase your experience with writing in a variety of forms, voices, and styles. As you nurture and develop your imagination through dream writing, your dreams and your writing become more compelling, vital, and alive. You find that dreaming and writing becomes intricately involved in your creative growth as you increase your familiarity with the literal, symbolic, mythic, and essential energy levels of your psyche that express your vital creative urge.

The following poem came from a visionary meditation on my Storm Troopers dream. It arises from my associations to the image of the storm from the original dream and focuses and expresses a vital emotional aspect of that dream and of the life event.

> Raging night,
> dream storms
> frigid
> shivers
> down my spine.
> I fall backward into time.
> Swept off my feet
> no longer certain what is mine.
> Foggy mourning
> swallows my heart,
> sends me weeping
> wretched wind
> pouring storm troopers
> like bullets from the sky

heaping leaping
cloaks of thunder wonder
bolts of lightening frightening
striking through
man-child's soul
with incomprehensible speed
he steps down
flying forward
toward some unseen destination
into forever's shroud,
hazel eyes locked shocked
inside an echo from the sky
gaze held permanently impermeable
within the icy water's reflection
of one seemingly innocent isinglass cloud
the icy water rose up
to embrace him
holding his lean
still warm body
wrapped
trapped
in its chilling embrace,
his spirit
fled,
fell
forever
forward
into
vast
open
space.

His beautiful body
ashes to ashes
delivered
itself
to those who had
borne him.
His soul continued falling
forever
forward
into
nonbeing

(NELSON, 1997)

As you begin to write, use the element to which you feel a strong emotional response as the springboard for your imaginative writing. This may be a visual image, emotion, sensation, or strong evocative word. I chose the word "storm." Hold a felt connection to the element that has energy for you. Close your eyes. Begin mindfulness breathing meditation if you want to. Envision the element you have chosen, feel the emotion, evoke it, and put words around it.

One way to start or continue writing is to use a phrase in conjunction with what has already been written as a springboard for what comes next. The phrase might be "What happened next was . . . " or "It was as if . . . ". Then continue writing. I used the springboard phrase "It was as if . . . "

THE WAY OF CREATIVE FORMULATION

In chapter 6, I talked about two ways to focus on dream material: the way of understanding and the way of creative formulation. The way of understanding is psychologically based. When it is a basis for intentional imagination writing, its purpose is to understand the meaning of the metaphor of the dream and how it reflects your life experiences as you extend the metaphor into poetry or prose that follow personal and collective themes. The reader can relate to your story by becoming emotionally involved with the plight of a character, or the suspense, or the twists and turns of the story. These psychological writings generally turn out in a way that can be understood. Even if the reader does not relate to the outcome, he or she can understand how it came about.

Intentional imagination writing that follows the way of creative formulation, on the other hand, expresses something unexpected. Something vivid and powerful develops as you intentionally and imaginatively expand, revise, and develop the original dream material. Creative formulation uses you as the vehicle of expression and yields writings that are often related to archetypal or transpersonal human experiences.

> Where the principle of creative formulation predominates, the material is continually varied and increased until a kind of condensation of motifs into . . . symbols takes place. These stimulate the creative fantasy and serve chiefly as aesthetic motifs. This tendency leads to the aesthetic problem of artistic formulation.[2]

You feel yourself compelled to write as you find yourself expressing nonpersonal, and thus transpersonal, motifs. Even when the plot and characters seem to be related to typical human experiences, there is some atypical, often numinous, quality embedded in your writing that seems to come from somewhere beyond what you have personally experienced. Such visionary writing seems to spring directly out of your imagination. You translate the essence of visionary writing into metaphors, poetic nuances, and word pictures that stimulate the sensory imagination and emotions of your readers so they can relate to them.

The level of experience and consciousness of your readers will partially determine whether they experience your writing as visionary as well as psychologically familiar. For some, visionary writing may seem mystifying and exciting; for others, it may seem obscure and difficult to understand because it touches upon something they have rarely or never experienced. What is written stretches their capacity to imagine or sense some reality beyond what is familiar, or what can be inferred from what is familiar. "When we turn to the visionary mode," Jung observes, "we are astonished, confused, bewildered, put on our guard or even repelled; we demand commentaries and explanations. We are reminded of nothing in everyday life, but rather of dreams, night-time fears, and the dark, uncanny recesses of the human mind."[3]

Jung seems to be of the opinion that visionary writing is "better" than psychological writing because it brings something "new" into human awareness. It is difficult, however, to draw a clear distinction between the two. Most creative writing is "psychological," with a touch or three of vision. If the piece informs or entertains some readers in some new way, it has a visionary component. If the piece does not bring anything new into the reader's awareness, it may serve to reinforce and perhaps clarify concepts and experiences. If you think you want to enlighten the whole of humanity, you risk setting yourself up for failure. Start with the goal of self-expression and trust that your form of expression will speak to others—if not all humanity, then some of it!

The strict difference between psychological writing and visionary writing, therefore, is that the former shares the stories and insights of personal and collective psychological experiences and the latter shares the stories and the insights of transpersonal, numinous experiences. Both styles of writing evolve from your ability to foster a relationship between your dreaming soul and your conscious intentional ego. The purpose of that relationship is to discover and maintain your inner vision and allow that vision to guide your creative urge into intentional outer form. Your creative impulse is expressed when you are enticed by some element in a dream to continue the story. The urge persists, insists, and pesters you until you express it in prose or poetry. Your creative urge takes over when your need for expression is so strong it captures your attention and excites your imagination. Your creative urge will strengthen as you increase your ability to express your ideas, images, and feelings. It "lives and grows in [you] like a tree in the earth from which it draws its nourishment . . . a living thing implanted in the human psyche."[4]

Your creative impulse is available to you through your dreams. In fact, your dreams reveal your creative process when you explore them with that intention in mind. The more you track your dreams and write with the right amount of conscious intention, the more you tune in to your creative urge and discover your unique voice and writing style.

YOUR VOICE AND STYLE

Your voice as a writer becomes evident as you develop your distinctive style and manner of expression. Your dreams help you clarify your voice and style, because they are formed from your unique way of experiencing and expressing your creative imagination. When you use the images and ideas that appear on the inner stage of your psyche to write prose and poetry, you build an imaginal bridge between your creative imagination and your intentional ability to write.

The kind of observation described in Exercise 22 will help you recognize your dreams as resources for further writing; it will help you recognize your own voice.

Exercise 22:
Voice and Style

Go over a series of dreams to help you to become conscious of repetitive themes and patterns that are not revealed in a single dream. Focus your intention on relaxing and meditating to turn your attention inward. Journal about what you notice. What is the tone of your dreams? What is the nature of the dramatic plots of your dreams? Are they love stories? If so, what kind? Write a thumbnail sketch of the plots and look for similarities and differences. What kind of personality style do you have in your dreams? Are you aggressive, passive-aggressive, passive, assertive? How about your characters? What is the emotional tone of their voices? Do they speak out loudly, or are they without voice? Dialogue with your characters to get a sense of them as aspects of your own psyche.

◆　◆　◆

Much of what you dream is what Jung refers to as an attempt of the stranger within to communicate with your conscious ego and redirect you out of complacency and into creativity. This stranger speaks to you in your dreams and can sometimes show you the way to solve difficult problems by changing your point of view and your attitude. Just as a series of dreams can reveal emotional themes, a series of prose and poetry writings based on dreams can, over time, reveal your communication style and voice. It is not necessary, however, for you to have many dreams recorded to discover your voice and style. Each dream gives you a glimpse. You may glimpse a *leitmotif*, or you may see the material for a fully fleshed out, finished product. Every additional dream contributes something new by adding various characters, themes, and plots. Your voice and style will become increasingly clear and distinct as you cultivate the tone and mood of your writing and become familiar with the dramatic structure of your dreams.

As you learned in chapter 4, the dramatic structure of your dreams becomes clear as you put words around the characters and the succession of events that take place in a setting or series of settings, each with an obvious emotional tone. Describe what you notice as the inner panorama of setting and detail opens and unfolds. Listen and catch the tone and words of the characters as they embody themselves and speak. Keep writing and the plot will develop, the characters will emerge, and the setting will unfold. Writing stories and poems from dreams involves weaving various parts of the imaginative theme into a pattern of unity. Jung believes it is absolutely necessary for you to be actively involved in this process, or else "the fantasy remains a flat image, concrete and agitating perhaps, but unreal [because the dreamer] . . . is not playing an active part."[5]

Respond to your curiosity and desire to put words around what you notice. Witness and give a voice to the emotions, images, actions, and themes that develop in your dreams. You may be inspired by an entire dream plot, or a single image, emotion, sensation, or word. When, as you write, you feel as if the narrative is composing itself and you are merely putting it into written form, you have found your voice.

When you write prose or poetry, your intentional conscious imagination works in partnership with your dreaming soul. They can be equally and cooperatively involved. Your ego works in the service of your dreaming soul. Try the following writing exercise to practice creating and interfacing visionary meditation writing with intentional writing based on dreams.

Exercise 23:
Creative Writing

Choose a dream and read it. Focus your intention on relaxing and meditating to turn your attention inward. Close your eyes and begin mindfulness breathing meditation. Visualize a mental memory image from the dream until you imaginatively reenter the memory of the dream. In the spirit of discovery, imagine and reenter the dream as you drop down into its emotions, images, and experiences. Feel yourself include your creative self in your composition as you reflect upon what happens next. Or take off from, "It was as if . . ." as a springboard to thoughtful associations to extend and expand the dream. Keep your pen writing on the paper without stopping, crossing out, or censoring what you write. Keep writing until the material begins to flow without intentional effort.

Put words around whatever images, ideas, or dialogue spontaneously emerge. Write as if the experience of the dream is continuing. Write whatever occurs to you, without censoring anything. Keep writing until you come to a natural stopping place. You may be on the edge of a cliffhanger, or on the verge of a resolution. You may want to write more or clarify what you have written at some other time. When you feel finished, stop for a while to allow your imagination time to replenish. If you push on and write when you are not feeling inspired, you risk losing the essence of your inspiration.

◆　◆　◆

DEVELOPING DREAM THEMES AND CHARACTERS

Your dreams have a plethora of themes and plots that you can use for creative writing. Practice advancing the plot of a dream in order to stimulate your imagination. This helps you develop writing skills. During visionary meditation, additional images and events usually develop from the original dream story. Through the theme, the dream shows what has been, what is, or what may be. The crisis presented in the dream and carried forward is often related to current, past, or future situations in your life. When the night dream stops, visionary meditation writing can continue to develop a possible course of action that could change the situation and affect your personal life. When you add intentional creative writing to the process, anything can and will happen!

Gradually, visionary meditation writing and writing an intentionally imaginative piece merges into writing that is no longer exclusively an extension of the dream. Your stories, in some sense, always reflect your personal development, but intentional writing shifts from restructuring past issues for healing to inventing future actual or fictional possibilities for fun! You accomplish this, in part, by allowing the flow of writing to continue until it comes to a natural end and nothing else emerges from the process. Even when nothing else happens, you may still be interested or emotionally drawn to the material. If so, you will want to continue.

> The point is that you start with any image . . . in your dream. Contemplate it and carefully observe how the picture begins to unfold or change. Don't try to make it into something, just do nothing but observe what the spontaneous changes are. Any mental picture you contemplate in this way will sooner or later change through a spontaneous association that causes a slight alteration in the picture. You must carefully avoid impatient jumping from one subject to another. Hold fast to the one image you have chosen and wait until it changes by itself. Note all these changes and eventually step into the picture yourself, and if it is a speaking figure at all then say what you have to say to that figure and listen to what he or she has to say.[6]

Creative writing is deliberate, but just as in a dream, often the current course of action ends with either an impasse or a resolution, and you still feel the urge to find out what could happen. This requires that you add more strategy to your composition process by thinking or wondering about the alternatives. If you write the story line a certain way, you discover what may happen. On the other hand, if you take the story forward in a different way, some other possibility could unfold. Put words around those possibilities until you feel you have come to an option that leads to a resolution, or to another stalemate.

A stalemate typically results in a crisis that is the high point of the dream or written drama. Opposing forces are usually in conflict. Keep writing, even if you are not certain about what you are writing, or if the writing works. You may start several different possibilities, leave them, and go on to another until you feel the one that says, "Yes! This is where the story wants to go." Stay with the process until something happens, something shifts, in the flow of writing. The result may be a clarification of a character, a change in setting, or a turn of events in the story.

Focus primarily on what you subjectively experience. Begin to blend that material with subtle, yet intentional, conscious ideas and images. The dream story will move forward in a spontaneous way that is still mostly experimental and uncontrived. You will feel inspiration from your dreaming soul and sense a connection with conscious ideas and images as the theme unfolds. Try Exercise 24 to focus more specifically on the unfolding of a theme or plot.

Exercise 24:
Writing for Theme and Plot

Choose a dream. Read it. Focus your attention on the theme or plot of the dream and the visionary meditation you have written. Focus your intention on relaxing and meditating to turn your attention inward. Close your eyes, begin mindfulness breathing if you wish, and allow the theme to develop by observing the inner flow of images, ideas, and metaphors. Follow the first inclination of your imagination while thinking about the direction the prose might go.

What about the theme grabs you? What happens next? Put words around what you see, feel, and sense. Let your visionary meditative imagination brainstorm with your intentional imagination, without censoring anything as you write.

◆　◆　◆

Whatever the dream presents, unless it is telepathic or precognitive, remember that it is often a compensation for a polarized or ineffective position in a life situation. Reflect on what the story would look like if it were written from a completely opposite perspective. The threatening antagonist may be a clue that you are overly optimistic or naive in an outer relationship. Or that you are not aware that you are threatening yourself or another person in some way. As you develop the theme through story writing, you may discover a change of position or an experience in the writing process that could lead to some new possibility for a story or poem and for a proactive change in your life. As you continue to expand the dream, invite the characters to participate.

One way to flesh out a dream character is to invite the character to have a conversation with you. Record and write down that conversation. Allow the characters to tell you about themselves, continue their monologue or dialogue in the dream, or put words around their role in the dream drama. Respond to them by taking on the role of the dream ego, or simply as a writer who is curious and wants to develop the character. The conversation will reveal and express a character's personality traits, intentions, and emotions. As those aspects of the character are fleshed out, the connection between the attributes of the character and the meaning of the situation in which he or she is participating begins to crystallize. You begin to understand how the dream is relevant to your life. You get to know the characters in the dream as though they were characters in your life, or characters in a novel.

Continuously shift back and forth between an objective position of studying the characters and a subjective experience of directly interacting with them, until you can do both almost simultaneously. It is helpful to ask several questions: Who are the people living in the dream? Who is the protagonist, the leading man or woman? Usually the dreamer is cast as the protagonist in a dream. That role is referred to as the dream ego. But sometimes the dream ego is the antagonist. If not, then who is the antagonist, the character who is usually in opposition or contrast to the leading man or woman (your dream ego)? Are there other characters that either support or are in opposition to the protagonist?

Study the characters and story line and write a descriptive sketch of each character and the roles they play. Pretend the characters are present. Ask questions. Write what they say. Who are they? What is their purpose? What emotions do they feel in the dream? How do they feel about what is going on in the dream? Allow the characters to continue a dialogue with you as you take the part of the dream ego from a conscious position.

It is worthwhile to listen, respond to, and encourage a spontaneous dialogue with each character in the story in order to learn more about them. Listen and respond, then listen again to the characters in your dreams. Trust the authenticity of their voices. Try not to over-control the direction of the conversation. Jung suggests talking to the people in dreams as a way of learning what they are about. "You must talk to this person in order to see what she is about and to learn what her thoughts and character are. . . . Keep your head and your own personality. . . . You can do that by stepping into the picture with your ordinary human reactions and emotions."[7]

When you have an imaginal dialog with the characters in the dream, you develop both the characters and the plot by allowing the characters to speak. They may even begin to interact with each other. Listen to them and respond by writing the conversation that evolves between the characters and/or the characters and your self. Establish an empathic relationship with each of your dream characters so you can understand what they feel. Let their feelings belong to them, as if they exist as separate people in their own right. They are created by your dreaming soul; they are part of your psyche; but relate to them as though they are real and separate people. "It is exactly as if a dialogue were taking place between two human beings with equal rights," Jung explains, "each of whom gives the other credit for a valid argument and considers it worthwhile to modify the conflicting standpoints by means of a thorough comparison or discussion."[8]

The characters in your dreams are the prototypes for the heroines and heroes of your personal and collective mythology. When they appear in your dreams, they resound with power as they act out the dramas of your life with enough mystery to puzzle and entice you. The ethnic and genetic history of your family of origin will help you recognize and understand how your collective heritage is represented symbolically in your dreams. You will have a good sense of the nature of certain archetypal dream characters. This knowledge will help you include those characters as qualities in your stories and poems.

Archetypal dream and story characters pull you into and engage you in emotional dramas from which you may awake feeling terrified—sobbing, screaming, laughing, or excited. A dream may tease you with a pun or terrify you with a grotesque image. When you wake up from a collective or transpersonal dream, you feel as though you have been involved in a sensational drama. Jung says that archetypal characters in dreams, "speak the language of high rhetoric, even of bombast."[9] Try the following writing exercise to focus on fleshing out personal dream characters.

Exercise 25:
Developing Personal Dream Characters

Choose a character that is active in a dream, perhaps one who acted in a theatrical manner and/or spoke persuasively and eloquently. The character may be you, as your dream-ego protagonist, or another character, as an antagonist. Focus your intention on relaxing and meditating to turn your attention inward. Close your eyes and focus on mindfulness breathing. When you notice any thoughts not related to the dream, bring yourself back and focus on your breath. When you feel centered, visualize the dream character doing what he or she was doing in the dream. If he or she was interacting with you, focus on that interaction. What was going on? What was happening in the story between the characters? Tap into the action of the story. What was the character doing or saying? What did the character look like? Conjure up a picture and meditate on the mental image of that character until you imaginatively reenter the memory experience of the dream. Let yourself drop and shift into visionary meditation as the dream begins to stir.

Listen and focus your awareness on that specific character at first. Observe the character do something or say something new. Or perhaps you, as your dream ego, will interact and/or talk with the character. Let the characters continue the story. Let them speak if they choose to and let your dream ego respond spontaneously. When you have finished visionary meditation, write what happened the same way you wrote the original dream—in first-person, fast-narrative style. You may want to record what happens on a tape recorder. Try this with each character in the dream.

When your writing comes to a natural stop, review what happened in the continuation of the dream story. First, think about each of the characters as they represent some aspect of your own psyche. What does the action or the dialogue of the characters tell you about you? What was their intention? What did they want you to know? What are they trying to teach you? Is there anything specific they want you to do? These questions help you clarify the purpose of the dream for your personal and transpersonal development.

Notice the style in which the characters talked and interacted with each other. When you describe this and write a dialogue from visionary meditation, you develop the ability to write dialog in prose and poetry.

◆　◆　◆

FLESHING OUT
TRANSPERSONAL CHARACTERS

When the characters in your personal dreams come to life in your prose and poetry writing, you find that your transpersonal dreams begin to come to life as well. Your transpersonal dream characters come from a place deep in your psyche that is beyond your personal and collective dreams. Like the mythical heroes of ancient times, they seem to glow with a numinous, creative, mystical energy. You feel the mystery and magic of these characters. They participate in extraordinary dream stories that give you a felt sense of a supernatural reality. That nonordinary energy that is presented by transpersonal characters is numinous energy. The root word of numinous—*numen*—refers to a presiding divinity or spirit of a place, a spirit believed to inhabit certain natural phenomena or objects. Numinous characters are highly charged with creative energy, genius, and an extrasensory existence.

When you have ESP dreams, you feel as though they come from that transpersonal realm, because you experience them as extraordinary. For instance, I experienced the telepathic dream Storm Troopers as extraordinarily numinous. I knew immediately that it was an extremely powerful and important dream, because my physical and emotional body was riveted during the dream and when I awoke from it. I felt, in the moment, an undeniable reality that I was experiencing something important. Although I understood how numinous and spiritual reality can manifest in a dream, I did not, at the moment of the dream, know that it foreshadowed the death of my future son-in-law. Later, I learned that his death, the time recorded on his death certificate, had occurred at exactly the time I was having the dream. It was not until I had told his parents about his death that I recognized how specific the dream metaphor had been in preparing me for both his death and my role in telling his parents about it.

Although transpersonal dreams are not necessarily extrasensory dreams, they do tend to have the aura of the supernatural about them.

When you flesh out the potency of a transpersonal dream character, it is always numinous and somehow beyond your personal ego. You feel these dream characters are transpersonal because they have a creative energy that stirs you in a way that is undeniable. As you practice story writing with transpersonal dreams, you become increasingly familiar with the *numen*, the spirit of creativity that lives within your dreaming soul. The following is an example of a dialogue I had with a dream character I encountered in a dream without a story, along with the associations it revealed to me.

The bridge to numinous reality, to engaging the essential energy of transpersonal experience, appears when I feel the breath of that beautiful or hideous dream character soft and warm and close to my ear. A shiver cascades, a not-so-subtle ripple, down my spine, alerting my senses to some invisible presence. I contain myself, remaining still as I breathe in sync with the soft warmth of the other. I can hear our breath mingling with my tingling skin. I open to embrace and be embraced.

Suddenly, I feel cautious. The breath becomes a whisper. "Don't come so trustingly into my embrace. Keep your eyes closed so you can make out my shady silhouette as I insinuate myself around you. No, I am not trying to frighten you. This caution I suggest is not about danger. It is about staying inside your own skin even as you shift to embrace my warmth. I am not here to harm you but I might accidentally assimilate you if you do not remain aware of yourself. The only risk to you is your desire to lose yourself in the mystery.

"That is better. Yes, I can feel the tautness of your skin now. Do not permit yourself to melt. This is not about losing yourself in magical reality. It is about visiting, experiencing, observing, and remembering and then returning to ordinary reality.

"It is odd, you know, this desire you have to leave what you call ordinary reality and enter what you call magical reality. I come to you because I need to give form to my reality. Without form, I wander endlessly, a ghost who is never seen, an essence that is never touched. I am constantly seeking form. I lust for corporeal reality. I hunger for the juiciness of your ordinary reality.

"And you hunger for the ethereal intangibility of my reality. Why is that? When you can throb with the passions of a lover and double over under the excruciating blow of betrayal? I long for the slicing bittersweet stench of ordinary reality."

Associations:

I can almost see the dream character now, or at least I imagine the form he is trying to take, and he is male. I keep my eyes closed as he suggests and I can sense him insinuating himself around me. I think about what he has said and about what he has asked. Why do I yearn to enter the ethereal realm of magical reality? Because magical reality is the realm of dreams and dreams are the spirits I do not know in my ordinary sensory reality. The dream spirits live on the other side of an almost invisible veil. They are concealed by shrouds of luminous light and eclipsed by shadows of their former selves. I feel them moving in the atmosphere, even though I cannot see them except in dreams or dream-like places.

We are taught that we must leave the dream place of magical reality by the time we are six or seven. Those of us who do not are the recipients of shaking fingers and worried frowns. We are sternly reproached for staring out the window and not paying attention to our lessons. "How will you ever learn to get along in the world if you do not learn your lessons?" Try as we may to return to the other side of the veil, we are pulled inexorably back into ordinary reality. Well-meaning family members and teachers take hold of any part of us that comes within their grasp and join forces to keep us anchored in their version of reality.

And so, as the years of our lives pass, we give up the struggle or consign the opportunities for magic to the night realm of our dreams. Dreams are of interest to some members of ordinary reality. Probably because everyone has dreamed, at least once, and, therefore, cannot deny having had a glimpse of magic. I intuit that the journey between the reality where dreams are born, and ordinary reality where they are manifested, is a template for the process of creativity. But, to safely visit the place of dreams, where magic lives, and fly back again into ordinary reality with some kernel of understanding about those otherwise unanswerable questions, I must regularly return and live within my own skin.

Try the following writing exercise to practice fleshing out your own transpersonal dream characters.

Exercise 26:
Developing Your Transpersonal Dream Characters

Focus your intention on relaxing and meditating to turn your attention inward. Choose a dream and a visionary meditation with a character that feels extraordinary, numinous, and mysterious. Assume it is a transpersonal dream. Begin mindfulness breathing if you want to and meditate for a while on the mental image, until you imaginatively reenter the memory experience of what you have already written.

Feel yourself shift back and forth between visionary meditation (where you visualize the numinous images, and characters) and intentional imagination where you give conscious thought to what you would like those characters to do. Focus on what you think you want to happen and the mental image, and notice what spontaneously emerges. Record or write the story of whatever happens. Keep your pen on the paper, or your fingers on the keys, until the energy of the numen is finished with you.

When the recording or writing comes to a natural stop, review what you have created and ask yourself what the characters told you about themselves. What was their intention? What did they want you to know? What are they trying to teach you? What do they want you to do? These questions clarify the purpose of the dream for your personal and collective transpersonal development as well as provide the foundation and scaffolding for the characters and plot of your story or poem. Then notice how they talked. When you write dialogue in intentional-imagination writing based on the style your characters use and the things they say, you practice the craft of writing dialogue for other forms of writing.

◆   ◆   ◆

The numinous spiritual quality of some dreams supports and reassures you as you explore the transpersonal dimension of your life. These experiences offer you the opportunity to have a direct experience of your soul. The soul is the central integral part, the vital core, the kernel of human consciousness and experience. Your dream is a gift of inspiration from your dreaming soul. It is intended to lead you to personal enlightenment and spiritual awareness. Your dreaming soul is your key and vital connection to inspiration and creative expression. Once you engage that inspiration and give it written form, the next step is to decide the best way to craft the material into prose and poetry.

In the tradition of depth psychology, the purpose of visionary-meditation writing is to expand dream material to gain personal insight. This is the way of understanding the meaning of the dream. Some dream writers stop writing when they feel that they have achieved some insight. If they continue to write, it may be difficult for them to tell when visionary meditation writing shifts into prose and poetry writing. The key is to continue to focus on and use the original dream material, until you naturally begin to diverge from the material and write in some form of crafted writing.

CRAFTED WRITING

As you become familiar with the presence of your dreaming soul, you hear your own creative voice. You discover your distinct style and begin to recognize the categories and forms of writing that come to you naturally. In the process of listening to your inner voice, you become familiar with what interests your imagination and the style with which your dreaming soul presents that material.

Each writer has a tendency and a talent to write in certain genres. These intentionally crafted forms of writing have a distinctive form, style, and content that ranges from scientific writing, journalism, and formal essays to personal memoir, story, and poetry. The content may be based on fact or fiction, reality or fantasy. Any of a plethora of basic archetypal themes that show up in dreams can serve as points of reference for a piece of writing and how it is crafted.

For example, dream-based writing may take the form of an essay or it may flow naturally into personal memoir, story, and poetry. When you intentionally notice and build upon the dramatic structure of your dreams, you discover more about the voice and style of your dreaming soul. You can express those aspects of your individual style through your intentional imagination and creative writing.

Writing a dream into another form of prose or poetry is a way to speak to the virtues and vices of people who share myriad experiences. Sometimes the reader can relate to what is written because it resonates with his or her own memories and experiences. Other times, the reader is intrigued by what is written because it stimulates interest and curiosity about a new concept or an unfamiliar experience. Or, it tells a story that draws the reader in to a fantasy experience that entertains or informs him or her.

Essay

When a dream sparks a contemplative response, it may lend itself to writing an essay about a particular theme or topic. A dream that causes you to continue to think about a particular issue may inspire you to write an essay. When you are invited by the dream material to convey your opinion or to inform or persuade another person about a matter of interest to you, your writing will likely take the form of an informal essay. Essays are most natural and effective when they are a thoughtful and personal interpretation of the meaning of the subject in which you are interested.

Personal Memoir

A personal essay or memoir is more than a record of your personal experience. It is a shift from dream and journal writing for personal development to a form that illustrates or explains a central theme or idea you want to communicate. Memoirs are likely to include anecdotes and/or characters from your dreams and personal experience that help the reader understand the central theme. To become engaged in a personal essay it is important for the reader to identify with the anecdotes and characters.

A memoir may begin with a memory, image, character, setting, or event in a dream that you transform through words that explain its meaning to you and, secondarily, to your reader. To write effective essays about personal experience, use vivid details that describe the characters, the action, and the setting. Think of the memory of the dream as a record of what happened that you want to recreate and elaborate. Make it so vivid that your readers experience it as though they were on the scene.

Why does the dream invite you to write a memoir? Does it remind you of a personal life experience? Did it lead you to a meaningful life experience? Use the cues: who, what, when, where, and why. Why do you remember this dream experience? Who are the characters in the dream, or of whom do they remind you? What does the theme express? What is the purpose of the memoir? What do you want your reader to understand as a result of reading this memoir? What other experiences have influenced the way you relate to this dream? To what period in your life does the dream relate? Where in your life did similar events occur? These cues help you remember and develop the important details you want to include in your memoir. Look for what this experience has in common with other personal experiences you have written about. Could this personal essay be transformed into a story or poem?

Suppose your dream-writing practice prompts you to write a story. At first, you write freestyle and rely on the inspiration that flows from the dream. This can lead you into writing prose fiction in a variety of forms. Prose fiction is any form of a story that continues the history of a dream character, or something that acts like a character (any potent image in a dream), through a story line. You develop and shape the plot that carries the story line by elaborating where, when, and how the people in your story live, what they do, say, believe, or think, and how they talk. You have to construct incidents in which your characters have the opportunities for psychological and physical conflict or activity. Your story may be tragic, comic, or satiric.

Slice-of-Life

Slice-of-life is a type of short story, novel, play, or film that is based on an extremely detailed, realistic presentation of a segment of life without evaluation by the writer. A dream can be thought of as a slice-of-life in that the writer is a spectator to the inner drama and has recorded that drama in detail as objectively as possible. The writer uses vivid detail to describe the environment, setting, and a specific situation, and the effect of those factors on the character or characters involved with it. Slice-of-life stories emphasize mood and atmosphere over action. They use carefully selected detail, careful characterization, and simple dialogue to build to an emotional peak. They may not have a traditional beginning, middle, and end, but they do have some plan in which a story character undergoes a change. The story makes a definite point, but may not come to a conclusion. The reader does not know what came before or what will come after the events of the story.

Vignette

A vignette is a very short story or literary sketch of about 300 to 600 words. This is an excellent form to use to practice the transition from story writing based on dreams to more crafted prose and poetry writing. Typically, a vignette is intended to convey an image or shed light on a character or specific situation. The writing style is succinct, exact, and intended to illustrate a point or principle. It may or may not have obvious beginning, middle, and end sections. Because a vignette has a poignant tone that may border on melodrama, it is especially compatible as a way to present the images featured in dream material.

Short Stories

A short, short story is about 500 to 1,500 words, and is based on a theme rather than a complex plot. Begin by choosing a dream theme that has energy for you and develop it into a story by giving it a clear beginning, a middle, and an end. Such a story works well if it conveys a bit of philosophy through a change that takes place in the attitude of one or more of the characters. The whole thing works even better if you can show that the change of attitude will be integrated into a character's overall philosophy.

If your dream material lends itself to a longer short story, it can be between 1,500 to 15,000 words, or from five to forty double-spaced pages. Both forms reveal a particular character by exploring a single major incident that takes place in a specific setting and in a limited time span, such as one day or one week.

Novella and Novel

If you are even more enthusiastic about where your dream story line can go, try for a novella or a novel. A novella is a long short story or a short novel, and, as such, may dip into the form of both. It may trace the development of a specific character or several characters through one or more situations. The novel is longer, because it invests more effort to imitate more people, places, and events found in real life. The transition from a short story to novella to novel happens as the writing traces the development of a character or characters through a series of incidents that continue over a longer span of time. You may begin with the characters and incidents of a dream or a series of dreams, and continue the story by adding twists and turns in the actions, speech, and thoughts of the characters that keep you engaged.

Poetry

Rather than attempt a synopsis of the intricate components of the art of writing poetry, I offer you the following example of a dreamlike poetic narrative form. This quote from *Galilee*, a novel by Clive Barker, illustrates the dramatic quality of dreams, prose, and poetry, and how they can be interwoven to express and capture the imagination.

> I dreamed again. This time I didn't dream of the sea, or of the gray wastes of a city, but of a bright burnished sky, and a wilderness of a desert. A little way off from me, there was a caravan of men and camels, its passage raising clouds of ocher dust. I could hear the camel drivers yelling to their animals, and the sharp snap of their sticks against the creatures' flanks. I could smell them too, even though they were a quarter of a mile from me; the pungent aroma of dirt and hide. I had no great desire to join their company, but when I looked around I saw that the landscape was otherwise empty in every direction.
>
> I'm inside myself, I thought; dust emptiness in every direction; that's what I'm left with, now I've finished writing.
>
> The caravan was steadily moving away from me. I knew if I lingered too long it would disappear from sight. Then what would I do? Die of loneliness or desiccation; one or the other. Unhappy though I was, I wasn't ready for that. I started toward the caravan, my walk quickening into a trot, and the trot into a run, as my fear of losing it grew.

Then suddenly, I was among the travelers; in the midst of their din and their stench. I felt the rhythmical motion of a camel beneath me, and looked down to see that I was indeed perched high on the back of one of the animals. The landscape—that aching void of baked earth—was now concealed from me by the dust cloud raised by travelers in whose midst I rode. I could see the backside of the animal in front, and the head of the animal behind; the rest was out of sight.

Somebody in the caravan now began to sing, raising a voice more confident than it was melodic above the general din. It was, I suppose you'd say, a dream song, wholly incoherent yet oddly familiar.[10]

This poetic prose illustrates how writing from a self-aware, first-person point of view can be used to develop setting, character, dialogue, and plot. The narrative entertains the reader with its attentiveness to detail as it draws you into the poetic mystery of an unfamiliar fantastical setting.

As you become familiar with what you experience during visionary imagination writing and intentional imagination writing, you can shift comfortably into each experience and use both in a sort of parallel process. You sense the difference between spontaneous images and those that you have chosen to create or develop intentionally. You appreciate and trust your writing voice and style. The experience of being and writing in each form gives you confidence. As you gain experience with writing in this way, you also gain insight and a deeper personal awareness that prepares you to write about your personal, collective, and transpersonal dreams and life experiences.

manifesting
your dreams

A work of art is not a human being, but is something supra-personal. It is a thing and not a personality; hence it cannot be judged by personal criteria. Indeed, the special significance of a true work of art resides in the fact that it has escaped from the limitations of the personal and has soared beyond the personal concerns of its creator.

—C. G. JUNG, *CW* 15, ¶ 108

The process of writing your dreams into your life leads to the goal of individuation. You develop and manifest your potential and consciously create your life. This final chapter presents a dream and follows it through all the phases of soulful dream-writing practice to illustrate how to put the process of dream and story writing together. As I was preparing to write it, I had a dream that I felt would work as an example of the process, and I was pleased that the dream content and the dramatic structure reflected one of my favorite forms of meditation—browsing in a bookstore. I use it now to illustrate how this dream-writing process flows from one phase to the next. As I illustrate the phases of dream-writing practice with my dream, I invite you to do the same with one of your own dreams.

Author Alan Gurganus describes the flow of writing from dreams and the way in which creative writing, when it is not literally based on dream material, is a conscious dream life. The essence of this dream-writing practice is writing and understanding dreams, using their images in creative writing, and tapping the source of the creative impulse to write conscious dreams that flow from your imagination when you are awake. "There's a strange combination in writing of using images and fragments from actual dreams," Gurganus notes, "but also finding a way to have a governed conscious dream life, which is what writing is. Which is what being an artist is. It's to have access to your own unconscious but also to direct it and be able to drag in facts and figures that you've found that please you: stories that you make up."[1]

PHASE I: MY ORIGINAL DREAM

In the first phase, I observe the literal and symbolic aspects of the dream and describe what I notice without embellishment. This is similar to brainstorming the first draft of prose or poetry. I write the main idea, image, or inspiration, without concern for grammar or style. I add my associations and amplifications at the end to explore what the dream symbolizes and how it illustrates an issue that has personal meaning for me.

I'm in an extremely large bookstore, like a warehouse, with many bins, tables, and shelves full of books. I'm delighted with all the possibilities. I wander around the bins reading titles on the backs of books for a long time. Then I remember that an author I'm interested in was in this store last night for a book signing. I had wanted to come, but could not. I can't remember his name or the name of the book. I look for it for a while, hoping it will be on display.

I drift beyond the front of the store through a mist into the back part of the build-ing. This area is arranged like a library, with shelves that go on and on as far as I can see. As I walk up and down the aisles of books, I'm fascinated because many of the books are bound in leather and seem to be first editions. Some of them appear ancient. I'm excited to be in this place. The atmosphere seems sacred to me and I feel at home as I browse. I wander back toward the front of the store and come to a shelf on the bor-der of the old and new book section. I think I see the book I have been looking for. I ask a young male clerk if the book is still available. He says he thinks there are a few left. He reaches up on the shelf and says, "Ah yes, here they are. I thought we had a few left." I see about three of them stacked up on the top shelf. He gets a wooden ladder, climbs up, and brings one down and hands it to me. I ask if the author signed it and he says no, but you can get him to sign it later. Now, I'm not sure if I want the book, but I look through it. The design is a leather-bound book attached to a hardcover book. I open the first part and read the first line, "This story is about events that happened in Santiago de Cuba." The young man says: "The story is pretty obscure unless you have a Jungian background. If you do, it is very valuable." I say I do, and I feel excited and decide to buy the book.

I am deeply involved in this dream when the phone rings. I remember that I felt the same way when I was deeply involved in my Storm Troop-ers dream and the phone rang. I feel disoriented by the sudden shift from dream to outer reality. I close my eyes and "get back in my body." I can feel the dream disappearing. I turn my sleepy attention to the phone and listen as my friend talks about his forthcoming trip to Cuba. The dream floods back. I tell my friend I will call him later. I grab my tape recorder, take several meditative breaths and describe the dream as I watch it replay on the inner stage of my imaginal memory. I feel as though I am back in the dream. I know how to keep a balance between the felt experience of the inner dream and the outer process of record-ing the dream. This balance is a crucial aspect of dream writing.

Next, I free-associate the dream to objective events in my life. Now and then, I ponder the possible subjective meaning in terms of how the dream may reflect what is going on in my psyche. I write down whatever thoughts I have without censoring them. Notice that I add the layer of subjective associations in the parenthesis as I write. This helps me catch a variety of associations and explore more than one theme at a time.

The Setting

I am in an extremely large bookstore, like a warehouse, with many bins, tables, and shelves full of books.

I have been writing *Night Wings*, a book about personal and transpersonal dreaming and creative writing from a Jungian perspective. I have read Jung's entire *Collected Works* and then some in the process. Talk about a big bookstore!

I love to explore bookstores, particularly old ones and ones with used books. They feel like walk-in treasure chests to me. Time always seems to disappear when I'm in a bookstore. As I am writing this book, it's as if part of me is constantly in a bookstore. Not only am I constantly browsing through the research I have done and the dreams I have analyzed, but this book is also like browsing because it is always in process. I love the process! I sometimes wonder if I will let it come to an end because I enjoy the writing and rewriting and researching so much.

In this dream, I focus on the specific goal of finding a specific book (making/finishing my own book?). I have been wandering around my inner bookstore all my life. I have been making this book for five years. I have been keeping a journal for thirty years. I learned to record my dreams and I learned how to write from male mentors.

I drift beyond the front of the store through a mist into to the back part of the building. This area is arranged like a library with shelves that go on and on as far as I can see.

Perhaps the mist symbolizes my inner work of making a transition from the literal and personal perspective of dream work into the historical and mythic perspective of the collective transpersonal unconscious. That "past" history of my deeper psyche is symbolized by the library, with shelves that go on and on as far as I can see. Treasures are available to me in the inner library/bookstore of my unconscious psyche. This book is building a bridge, for me and hopefully for others, through the mist of unfamiliar and unexplored regions of the psyche into the conscious, imaginative expressiveness of the creative psyche.

I open the first part and read the first line, which says, "This story is about events that happened in Santiago de Cuba."

Why Cuba? I've been fascinated by Cuba since the late 1950s. I have several friends who left Cuba as young men because of the revolution. But why Santiago de Cuba? I don't think I've ever heard of that town before. Does it exist? I have three male friends who are associated with Cuba. Two of them were born there, and the other made a movie and CD of Cuban music. The two who were born there were affected by Castro's revolution. Why Santiago? I'll do some research about that city.

Perhaps this part of the dream symbolizes the part of my psyche once isolated from seeing myself as a writer. Until I was inspired to write *Night Wings,* I had been "ruled" by the tyrant of fear of writing because I am not schooled in the rules and regulations of literary etiquette. But *Night Wings* insisted on being written. So I wrote it from my heart, even though my style and/or my skill may be homespun.

Dream Characters

I remember that an author I'm interested in was in this store last night for a book signing. I had wanted to come, but could not. I can't remember his name or the name of the book. I look for it for a while, hoping it will be on display.

The male author in the dream is an aspect of my animus that has developed the ability to manifest inner awareness in the outer world as this book. I'm the author and my own signature will come when I complete this book. Perhaps the book in the dream symbolizes the knowledge and understanding I have developed over the years. That awareness stimulates this creative work of writing. I'm excited by the book I have found in this dream, and I'm eager to learn from it. I am certainly excited with the process of writing this book! It has, in a way, brought me out of the mist of my work with dreams into a form of clarity.

I ask a young male clerk if the book is still available.

At first, I try to find (make/write) this book all by myself. I do not have the title (the title for this book), or the author's name (my own voice is becoming known to me only as I write). I spend a lot of time wandering around (brainstorming and revising). When I ask for guidance, I'm given some of what I need (I hire a copy editor, I ask a couple of people to read the manuscript and give me feedback). Good that I let myself ask for help. That works, I get what I need when I ask and I learn a lot. (The young male clerk, another animus figure, is an aspect of my inner masculine who can help me discriminate and find what I am looking for.)

Dream Plot

"The story is pretty obscure unless you have a Jungian background. If you do, it is very valuable." I say I do, and I feel excited and decide to buy the book.

Dream words are always important. They are speaking to me in a direct manner. Perhaps this message supports my decision to provide the Jungian background in *Night Wings* so my readers can integrate psychological healing and creative development into the dream-writing process. At first, I wanted to write only about intentional imagination and creative writing, because I was excited by the idea that passive imagination, active imagination, and intentional imagination all have the dreaming soul as their source. I was searching for a path that I could use to access that source for my own creative writing. But once I got started writing *Night Wings*, I was compelled to include the Jungian background.

Dream Symbols

The design is a leather-bound book attached to a hardcover book.

Why leather-bound and hardcover combined? The leather-bound comes first, so that suggests it precedes the hardcover. I'm not sure what that means. Leather-bound suggests old, valued, wise information. Perhaps it is a journal. Perhaps it refers to the value of all my years of journal writing, dream writing, expressive writing, and creative writing, as a foundation for this work. Hardcover suggests a completed work that is other than a journal. It is more public—a book that is read by others. But since it is attached to the journal, perhaps it represents the journal/dream writing as the jump-off material that interfaces with my expressive creative writing.

PHASE 2:
VISIONARY MEDITATION WRITING

After I feel complete with my associations, I shift into visionary meditation writing. I encourage my passive imagination to allow the energy of the dream material to develop further. When I sense that the story is continuing, I write what I notice to help flesh out the symbolism and personal mythology of the dream. I follow the unfolding metaphor to find out how it relates to my personal and collective mythology.

One of my most valued dream mentors, Dr. Stanley Krippner, describes personal mythology:

> Your personal mythology is the loom on which you weave the raw materials of daily experience into a coherent story. You live your life from within this mythology, drawing to yourself the characters and creating the scenes that correspond to the guiding theme. A great deal of this activity occurs outside of your awareness. To discover and transform your mythology is one of the most empowering choices open to you.[2]

Through visionary mediation writing, I flesh out the themes and characters to amplify the mythic story quality of the dream. I gently allow the setting, images, and characters to develop outside the original dream, guiding them as they do so. Here is an example of visionary meditation writing based on the dream described in phase I.

I purchase the book, leave the store, and find a place where I can settle in to read it. I feel as if I have a new treasure waiting to be explored. I walk across the street to a park and sit down under an old pine tree. I settle my back against the mature trunk, pull the book from the bag, and hold it on my lap. What a curious design. The soft, worn, leather-bound part of the book appears to be an old journal. It is attached to a modern hardcover section. This gives me the impression that the journal has been extended or written into a book for the publication I have just purchased.

I feel a thrill of excitement as I stroke the soft leather. I open the cover and my heart leaps at the sight of the neat yet ornate hand-written script. I am ready to be carried away and join the journey this man has written about.

FEBRUARY 11, 1916

Today is my sixteenth birthday. I'm sitting in the middle of an ancient grove of piñon trees that have stood on the top of this hill overlooking the vast sea that surrounds me far longer than I have been alive.

When I was still an infant, my Afro-Cuban nanny often carried me up here wrapped tightly within a soft woven shawl that my nose still remembers. We shared many moonless and moon-full nights in the company of her Candomblé companions. My first memories of those nights are a combination of dreams and experiences that continue to live in my body and my soul. I can drift back to those times and feel the pulsating rhythm of drums and the enthralling cadence of voices chanting as though I were still cradled in that soft cotton sack hanging against her breasts. I can feel her heartbeat increasing as she moves to the rhythm of the drums. She and her people communicated with their gods through the drums.

I have been coming here alone since I was six years old. I come whenever I need to soothe my soul, speak with my God, or excite my imagination. I hike up to this grove of ancient piñon trees and sit beneath the one that has always sheltered me and given me strength. This tree and I have both grown stronger and taller over the years. Together we have met the challenges of stormy weather. It seems as though we have looked out to this vast cerulean sea together for many lifetimes.

It is fitting, I think, for me to begin this journal that marks my sixteenth year with a brief summary of my life so far, because soon I will be a man.

This is fun! It reflects my personal and collective mythology as a developing story writer. This brief visionary meditation writing leads me to the next phase of my dream-writing practice. I am inspired to continue with the direction the dream material is already taking. I feel reinforced and invited by the flow of my writing to continue the process of working with this dream as an illustration for writing prose and poetry from dream material.

PHASE 3: CREATIVE WRITING AS INTENTIONAL IMAGINATION

Intentional imagination is the phase in which I purposefully play with what I have written based on the dream and see if it lends itself to becoming a story (or a poem). This process of taking the material beyond the dream is like revising and expanding any written form of prose or poetry. It is an ongoing process of responding to a spontaneous flow of images, ideas, and characters and then editing and revising that flow. When I write intentionally, I become more focused upon molding the dramatic structure of the material. I attend to and direct several possible themes and resolutions of the story that either emerge from the dream material or materialize out of my intentional imagination.

Here is an example of a dream-inspired intentional imagination story based on my bookstore dream.

FEBRUARY 11, 1916 (CONTINUATION OF JOURNAL ENTRY.)

My name is Luis William Madueano. I was born here in Santiago de Cuba, at the turn of the century, on February 11, 1900. My father, Antonio Marcellino Madueano, is a prominent protestant minister and missionary. My mother, Alma Kale Madueano, seems to enjoy being a minister's wife, though I think that is mostly because she loves to entertain and travel to foreign missions. She is of French-English descent and was born in Vermont. When she came to Cuba on a mission as a young woman, she met my father. They married and she settled efficiently into his life. I think Alma considers her children to be a necessary part of her role as a minister's wife. She has never seemed particularly interested in either my sister or myself. Don't get me wrong; she has always been kind. She is a woman of God, but no one would call her a warm, affectionate woman.

My father, Antonio, is a pleasant enough fellow. I rarely see him. When he is around, he reads and works on his fire-and-brimstone sermons. He can enchant an audience, truly he can! I think his charisma developed as a result of the suffering he endured as a child. He was born with a dreadful facial deformity that made it impossible for him to speak. He suffered through many operations. The local churches raised money to have his jaw reconstructed several times. He had several plastic-surgery procedures to rebuild his jaw and lower face. They left him with an odd speech pattern that I believe contributes to his charisma and his ability to mesmerize his congregation.

My sister, Lucia, adores Papa. She is his "darling." She is six years older than I am and never lets me forget it. When she gets angry with me, she goes running to Papa. Consequently, I keep my distance and avoid her as much as possible.

My nanny, Blanca, is like night compared to day in the ways in which she is different from my family, yet she has been and continues to be the one person I feel close to. Nanny Blanca is a tall, thin, swarthy woman who allows her long, wavy, dark-brown hair to flow loose when her workday is done. She stays in a small room at the back of our house. I wouldn't say she lives there, because she has very few possessions. Although, when I was younger, she choreographed most of my day- and nighttime activities, I always had the sense that she actually lived somewhere else. Yet when I was a child, she seemed to appear whenever I needed her. (Actually, she still does, although I see her less often now that I am older.)

When I was a child, Blanca made sure to present me to my parents at the appropriate times. I usually had tea with my parents and my sister in the morning after breakfast. Most days, I shared lunch and supper in the kitchen with Nanny Blanca. Each evening, when my parents were at home, I sat with them for fifteen minutes after supper and listened to my father read from the Bible. Another ten minutes or so were given to instructing me in the ways of righteousness and compassion, after which I would dutifully kiss Mama and then Papa on the right cheek and be taken off to bed by Nanny Blanca.

I doubt that my parents know to this day about the adventures I frequently shared with Nanny Blanca after we left the warm security of their pious parlor. Nanny had been raised by her godmother, who taught her the mysteries and magic of the original African Candomblé societies. So my Nanny Blanca could see things that ordinary people could not. She could speak with the dead. I can't imagine that my parents knew she practiced the rituals of Candomblé magic. But the music, drumming, dances, and rituals were a regular part of my childhood.

As I write this text, spontaneous images and ideas begin to flow that give the story a life of its own that is completely separate from the original dream. At this point, in this particular piece of writing, I realized I need to do some research to find out historical data about Cuba. The following piece is a preliminary sketch, written as part of Luis' journal, that illustrates how to include research. Below, I illustrate how I wrote it into a preliminary draft to integrate it into the story as it develops.

An Entry in the Leather-Bound Journal by Luis W. Madueano, written in 1962: In 1933, Batista y Zaldivar was 22, one year younger than I, when he became Cuba's dictator. He held the position until 1940. Batista was the president of Cuba between 1940 and 1944, and between 1954 and 1958. His regime was considered corrupt and authoritarian.

He was overthrown on New Year's Day, 1959 by a revolutionary movement led by Fidel Castro, who established a socialist state. Castro had supported other liberation struggles in Latin America and Africa and maintained close ties with the Soviet Union. When Victor was born in 1941, Batista had just become president. But I am getting ahead of my story.

In 1957, when Victor was sixteen years old, Fidel Castro had been organizing a revolution to take over the Cuban government. Victor was still very young and, although he realized his small island home was in the midst of an oppressive political conflict, he had not yet been personally touched by the struggle. As my edu-

cated but well-protected son, he had little awareness, concern, or understanding of the ramifications of the political struggle that Cuba was facing.

Victor had grown up as my only son. I am of Spanish and French-English descent and, of course, I took up the ministry like my father. I married the beautiful blonde Spanish flamingo dancer, Sophia Antonia de la Cruz. She bore me one daughter and one son. Sophia was much like my own mother in that she was not overly domestic or motherly.

She was quite happy to leave most of the tending of the children to Nanny Blanca, who cared for me and my sister when we were children. I love Nanny Blanca. We had many mysterious adventures with her Candomblé companions. It is natural that she should have a part in raising my daughter and my son. She took a special interest in Victor, so I'm certain he, too, has become familiar with Candomblé magic.

Nanny Blanca was forty-six when Victor was born. By then, she was a well-established and highly sought after practitioner of Candomblé ceremonies around Santiago de Cuba. She taught Victor, as she taught me, much more than either of us realized about that ancient African tradition. The Candomblé were distinguished by their passionate indigenous gods, dances, and magical energy. I was fascinated by her stories when I was a child, and I am sure the mysteries I experienced in her presence have somehow enlightened my ministry. Even though her Candomblé rituals are considered pagan by many, I have always felt they were essentially an expression of the divine.

Perhaps Victor's early experiences with these mysteries have aroused his desire to be a poet rather than a minister. Is there really much difference between a poet and a minister?

Anyway, by the time Victor was sixteen he preferred to believe he was related to a former poet laureate of Cuba due to a brief but passionate dalliance of his grandmother's, my mother, with said poet. (If this is true, Victor knew more about my mother than I ever did!) Be that as it may, the boy had always cherished the fantasy that he, too, would one day achieve such an honor. I, of course, wanted him to follow in my footsteps and my father's footsteps and become a minister.

But Victor apparently had no calling to God. He was drawn to the worldly experiences of the senses and the emotions. As a boy, he loved to wander the hills and caves around our home. He would often disappear for hours on one adventure or another. When he was a young man, he attended university, where, despite my passionate protests, he studied literature and political science. He believed the two were related and would be important areas of knowledge for his future.

As I continue to write, I increase and hone my intention to develop, shape, and mold the partially formed material into a specific form that may or may not be related to the original dream. I grasp the original material, like a lump of partially formed clay. I manipulate and sculpt it as I experiment with imposing a specific form upon the material, without the intention of staying close to the original dream, but still allowing the story to spontaneously unfold. I keep in mind what Jung says about the poetry of dreams: "The poet now and then catches sight of the figures that people the night-world—spirits, demons, and gods; . . . feels the secret quickening of human fate by a suprahuman design, . . . has a presentiment of incomprehensible happenings in the pleroma."[3]

When I write prose and poetry based upon dreams, I want to develop the dream material so that others can relate to it. I am no longer exploring the original dream for my own edification. Now I am intentionally giving my imagination *carte blanche* to create whatever form flows. The following story is what unfolded. (It seems to actualize the personal meaning of my original dream, which was guiding me to move from thinking about intentional imagination writing to doing it!) Now my imagination is engaged in the story that definitely has a course of its own that I had not plotted out in advance. I love the feel when writing is flowing in this way.

The story opens on the hillside overlooking the northern coastline of Cuba just above Santiago de Cuba. Victor, a young man of sixteen, is wearing a straw hat that covers his sandy blonde hair. Dark sunglasses shade his hazel-blue eyes. His blue jeans, soft flannel shirt, and denim backpack match the uniform worn by affluent adoles-

cents throughout the world in 1957. He walks confidently along a dirt footpath that snakes ahead of him, winding along the edge of the hill. The path disappears around a bend in the distance. The intense sun shines high in a cloudless blue sky. He removes his sunglasses, turns his head to the right, and looks down at the vast turquoise sea. Pelicans soar below him above the sparkling sea.

He smiles as he holds his right hand over his eyes and marvels at the formation they create with such efficiency. The movement of their powerful wings as they pump to catch the wind, find a current, and coast along a wave of air creates a pattern that undulates across the open space like a single-winged entity.

He turns away from his study of the pelicans to search the landscape in front of him. About 100 yards ahead, at the very top of the hill, he sees the familiar grove of piñon trees. He puts his sunglasses on and heads down the path toward the turn off, where he must climb the steep, rutted path leading to the grove. As he picks up his pace in anticipation, he is excited about an idea he has for a new poem.

He makes the steep climb easily in his well-broken-in hiking boots. He reaches the top of the hill, bends over to catch his breath, then steps eagerly onto the narrow path that leads to the interior of the grove. No premonition flickers across his mind as he settles into the well-worn indentation at the foot of a large piñon tree where he often sits to dream and write. He sighs happily as he leans back against the tree and opens his backpack. He pulls out the leather notebook and pen, both gifts from his father. His pen poised over a fresh blank page, he closes his eyes.

"Formation," he muses. He opens his eyes and begins to write. "A group of individuals agreeing to coordinate their efforts to achieve something that cannot be done by only one. This makes me think about that ancient conundrum of the individual vs. the collective. What value does the formation have to the pelicans? Why do they cooperate and form a unit that spreads across a piece of sky and rolls along the pattern of the air current? It must serve survival in some way."

> *Pelicans soar along the invisible current*
> *innocent turmoil beneath their wings*
> *still flows the rainbow serpent*
> *toward a future yet unseen*

Gunshots startle him out of his reverie. He closes his notebook and quickly returns it to his backpack. "What the hell is that!" he mutters aloud as he peers through the cover of the trees. Two men are walking on the path leading into the grove. They are intensely focused on their conversation. Victor hooks the backpack over his right shoulder and steps behind the tree where he can observe the men without being seen. They walk right up to the opposite side of the tree and stop.

"I think we're safe in here for the moment," the tall, powerfully-built man says quietly.

"I don't think we should hang around for long," the smaller man responds.

"Of course not, but we have to decide what to do next."

"I think we should bury the body right now! We can drag him in here and bury him and he won't be found for a while. That will give us time to finish our assignment and get off this damn island. I'm sick to death of the way this place smells."

"I'm not so sure," the large man replies. "If we get off the island, it won't matter if his body is found. In fact, it could work in our favor by diverting attention away from us. That will give us time to finish our job in Santiago. While Batista's strong-arms are looking for whoever shot him, they will focus their investigation here, on the island, for a while. That will give us time to get to Florida and disappear."

Victor is alarmed. His thoughts are racing. "I think I have just witnessed a murder! Why are they talking about Batista? They speak English! Could they be working for Castro? Or are they CIA agents? Oh, shit, I don't want to know about this!" He freezes as he realizes that, if he is discovered, he will be killed. He can feel his heart beating rapidly and the blood pounding in his temples. He takes a deep silent breath and waits as he tries to calm his fear.

The two men walk back down the path and are soon out of Victor's sight. He thinks, "What am I going to do? I can't pretend this didn't happen, but I don't want to get involved."

Without actually deciding what he intends to do, he creeps down the path and follows the men. At the edge of the grove, he peers down the footpath and watches them as they disappear around a curve on the hillside. His forehead furrows with a deep frown as he trudges after them, his head bowed in concentration on the path just in front of his feet. Red-black streaks in the dirt pull his eyes along a track that leads into some shrubs to his right. Despite his fervent desire to remain uninvolved, his feet follow the track into the foliage. Just on the other side of a tall hibiscus plant, he comes across the body of a man lying face down in a pool of blood. The man is wearing a rumpled and dirty khaki uniform like those worn by members of Batista's army.

Victor reaches down and pokes the man's shoulder. No response. He stands there for a moment and then realizes the two men are getting away. He is repulsed as he turns the body over. Three bullets have pierced through the back of the dead man's head and destroyed his face beyond recognition. Victor searches the body for identification. He uses his handkerchief as he removes and opens the dead man's leather wallet. A picture of Juan de la Cruz causes his heart to skip a beat. "I know this man! He is a friend of my father. Oh, my God," he sighs and pushes the wallet back in the dead man's pocket. He turns the body back over on its face and backs out of the bushes.

He doesn't know what he should do or what he wants to do, but he feels pulled to follow the two men. Time and circumstances will lead him to what he is meant to do. He picks up his pace so he will get around the bend before they get too far and he loses sight of them.

As he follows the men, he is at first careful to stay far enough behind so they won't see him if they should happen to turn around. But he becomes absorbed in his own inner conflict and forgets to keep an eye on them. He is startled by the sound of their voices, and he abruptly comes upon them sitting under a tree on the side of the path. They stand up when they see him, glancing at each other. The smaller man puts his hand under his vest. Victor is certain he is reaching for the gun. "So he is probably the one who actually killed Juan," Victor thinks. For a moment, he almost panics. He feels his muscles tighten, ready to flee. But he forces himself to appear calm and says:

"Buenos días, señores, cómo estás ustedes?" He smiles broadly.

"Bien, gracias, y usted?" They respond in concert, staring at him intently.

"Bien, bien," he nods, and starts walking down the path.

"JUST A MOMENT PLEASE!" the large man shouts.

Victor turns around slowly, trying not to show his fear. "Si, señor, hay problema?"

"Do you speak English?"

"Yes, I do."

"Good, that will help. You see, we don't know how to get back to town and we have an important meeting there this afternoon. Perhaps you could help us get to town as soon as possible?"

Victor thinks quickly. The last thing he wants is to hang around with these guys. But on the other hand, he is the only witness to the murder of Juan de la Cruz. Besides, he had better not upset these guys; he could get himself killed!

"I'm headed back to town myself. You're welcome to come with me. I have to hurry, though. I am late for class."

"Great," the large man's smile reveals long pointed incisor teeth. "Thanks a lot." The two of them fall into step behind Victor as he heads toward the outskirts of Santiago.

As he leads the killers along the path, Victor contemplates what to do. If he plays innocent, perhaps he can leave them at the hotel, go on his way, and forget this entire revolting incident. "I am a poet, after all," he tells himself. "I'm not temperamentally suited for this kind of thing. Politics and power don't interest me except from a literary perspective." But the intellectual world of the university is a far cry from the reality that he is right now facing. At this exact moment, he is leading two men who have just murdered a close friend of his father's into the heart of Santiago.

As they walk, the larger man asks: "What's your name?"

"My name is Victor." He responds purposefully, neglecting to add his surname "And yours?"

"I'm George, and this here is Jack," the man responds.

Victor does not comment. He does not want to encourage familiarity.

"You speak good English, how come?

Victor thinks: "Better than yours, mister." But aloud, he says: "My grandmother was born in the United States."

"Oh, married a Cuban did she?"

Victor does not respond.

"What were you doing up in the hills?" the man asks with a slight rumble in his voice.

"Oh, I go up there often," Victor says attempting to keep his voice calm. He points to the backpack. "I'm a poet and I hike around these hills for inspiration."

"Were you inspired today?" the man asks slyly.

"I'm always inspired," Victor hedges.

"What inspired you today?"

Victor's mind raced. "The pelicans."

The man snorts: "You were inspired by those dirty birds?"

"Well, seen from above they don't seem dirty," Victor muses.

"Well, from where I stand, they just eat a lot of crap on the wharfs and streets. They are nothing more than glorified pigeons. In fact, I use them for target practice. That's what we were doing up there in the hills."

"You were shooting pelicans?" Victor can't keep the incredulity out of his voice.

"Yeah, didn't you hear the gun shots? You must have been near by."

Victor takes a deep breath. "No. When I am writing, I am completely absorbed. A gunshot could go off right next to me and I wouldn't hear it."

"Humph," the man snorts. "Poets . . . you're all lost in space if you ask me. Better be careful, son. These are dangerous times and a poet could get himself killed by not paying attention to what's going on around him. How about reading us your poem about pelicans," he snorts.

Victor ignores him, but he hears the not-so-veiled threat in the skulking man's voice as they arrive in front of the Hotel de los Americas. "Well, here you are. You should be able to find your way from here. So long!" He hurries off down the street. As he turns the corner, he looks back and sees that the two men are standing and watching him. He waves and they wave back. Victor is relieved when they are out of sight. He stops and leans against the building, taking some deep breaths to calm himself. He edges his way back to the corner and looks around just in time to see the two men walk through the main entrance to the hotel lobby.

"Now, what am I going to do?" he asks himself. "Juan is dead. I know who killed him. I have to do something, but what?"

Victor makes his way through the crowded streets to the other side of Santiago. He lives with his parents and his older sister at the old Spanish colonial mansion that is now the protestant mission. As he enters the house, he has an impulse to tell his father everything. He would feel better if he turned the burden of what to do over to his father. He hurries down the long, cool hall to his father's study. As he approaches the solid oak door, he hears a man's voice. "But Reverend Madueano, you and your family are in danger. You must get out of Cuba at once! There is no time to waste."

Victor creeps closer to the door. "Batista will be overthrown any day now. Already Castro's terrorists have assassinated his top officials. Batista is at this moment being smuggled out of Cuba and if you know what is good for you, you will get out now while you have the chance."

"I will not leave my congregation," Luis replies. "They depend on me to keep them close to God. I will not abandon them in their hour of need."

Victor runs to his room and sits on the arm of a large overstuffed chair. He dumps his backpack into the chair and rests his head on his hands. "What am I going to do? I'll have to tell father. That's all I can do; I can't manage this all by myself." He runs quickly down the hall and slips into the open library next to his father's study. He sees a man, who wears a uniform exactly like Juan's, pass by the door. "Suit yourself. But remember I warned you!" The man declares as he leaves the room.

He paces back and forth several times, and then resolutely walks from the library to the open door of his father's study. He enters and finds the study empty. "He's gone!" Victor shouts as he runs out of the room and down the hall hoping to catch his father before he leaves the mission. His father's car is just pulling out of the gate when Victor gets to the front door.

He turns and runs back down the hall to the kitchen, where his mother is instructing Lepiota about preparations for the evening meal.

"Mama!" he exclaims. "Where is Papa going? I must talk to him immediately! It is very important that I speak to him at once!"

Señora Madueano smiles indulgently at her only son. How handsome he is with his unique combination of Spanish and French/English looks. He is such a passionate young man. "Your father has gone to an important meeting at the Hotel de Los Americas."

As Victor turns and runs back down the hall, yelling, "I have to stop him!" his mother calls out, "I don't think you should disturb him, son, this is a very important meeting."

"I have to get to the hotel quickly Mama, Papa's life may be in danger!" He runs through the front door, jumps on his bicycle, and takes off down the road racing after his father's car.

By the time Victor makes his way through Santiago to the hotel, his father, whose car has been impeded by heavy traffic, has just entered the building. Victor sees that his father's car is empty. He can feel his heart racing, his muscles tense as he turns and races to the hotel entrance. But he realizes he will have a better chance of helping his father if he is composed. He forces himself to slow down and walk calmly through the front door. On the far side of the lobby, Luis is shaking hands with a man wearing the familiar khaki uniform. Victor scans the room quickly. Once, twice, and on the third pass, he sees the two men standing in the shadow of a corner looking at his father. The small man, Jack, has his hand under his vest.

Victor pushes his way through the crowd to his father's side. "Papa, an emergency, Mama has had an accident. You must come home right now!" His father slowly turns his head toward Victor with a slightly annoyed but quizzical look on his face. Over his father's shoulder, Victor can see Jack removing his hand from his vest. He grabs his father's hand and pulls him across the lobby.

Reverend Madueano shouts, "Victor what are you doing! Stop this right now, this is an important meeting!" Just then, the gunshot explodes, and Victor and his father look back to see the man in khaki fall to the floor. The Reverend moves quickly then. "Victor, hurry, but be calm." They leave the hotel, run to the Reverend's car, jump in, and screech away from the building just as Jack and George come through the front door. They watch as the Reverend's car disappears down the street. They shrug, and look at each other with eyebrows raised.

Jack says, "Let's get outta here." They take off running and disappear around the next corner.

Meanwhile, driving as fast as possible back toward the mission, Luis glances at his son. "What the hell is going on? Tell me everything, Victor."

Victor tells his father what he saw and heard at the top of the hill. He describes the man he found murdered and his tortuous hike back to Santiago with the killers.

The Reverend is quiet for a long time. Then he sighs, "You are a brave man, my son. Now you will have another opportunity to test your courage. When we get home, I want you to pack a few essentials, don't forget your Bible, and be ready to leave in five minutes. Your mother and I are prepared for this. Just do exactly as I tell you."

"What are we going to do Papa?" Victor whispers.

"We are leaving Cuba," his father says sadly.

"Leaving Cuba! But Papa, I don't want to leave! What about the mission? There must be another way to deal with this!" Victor is astounded. His father would never leave Cuba. He has always refused to consider it; always sworn he would not leave his mission.

"You and your mother and sister are more important than the mission, than God's work, than our home, and even more dear to me than Cuba." Luis jerks to a stop in front of the mission door. "Now hurry and be back here at the car in five minutes! Not a minute longer, Victor! Our lives depend upon getting out of Cuba immediately!"

Victor runs, thankful for his long, powerful legs. In his room, he stops for a full minute and looks around. How can he decide what is essential? He has lived his entire life in this room, in this house. It is full of his possessions, full of his memories. He shakes his head, "No, I can't be sentimental now." He throws his straw hat on the bed and replaces it with a dark blue wool baseball cap. He grabs his knife and compass, a box of matches, a sweatshirt, jacket, and a pair of leather gloves and stuffs them in his backpack. He adds his sunglasses, reading glasses, a stack of his personal journals, including an empty one, and a handful of pens. Just before he leaves his room, he stuffs a copy of the poems of Pablo Neruda into the pack. He is glad he was wearing his hiking boots already. He runs down the hall, then turns, runs back to his room, and pulls the picture of his mother, father, sister, and him from the frame by his bed. He stuffs it in the sack as he runs back down the hall to the steps leading to the ground floor.

Victor arrives just as his Mother is opening the car door. She turns toward him and smiles wanly. Victor feels a lump in his throat when he sees her tears. He hugs her quickly and whispers urgently, "We'll be okay, Mama. Let's go!" Victor shouts to his father as he climbs into the back seat.

Tires squeal as his father speeds down the mission driveway and turns onto the main highway leading to the airport. Victor is tense; his heart is beating wildly. But he resolves to remain calm. "Think of this as an adventure!" he tells himself. Suddenly, he thinks about his sister. He is glad she is already safely off the island, visiting relatives in Vermont. Besides, it would be a real pain to have to deal with her under these circumstances!

He pulls the blank notebook out of his backpack and begins writing furiously. He feels an urgent need to describe the events that are shattering the world as he knows it. "The only way I will get through this is if I treat these changes as a story that I'm making up. That will make this bearable."

I wrote this rough draft, which became the length of a short story (3,583 words), to illustrate how to use dream material as a springboard into a story. Contemplate the memory and energy of the dream and the visionary meditation, and let what wants to happen, happen. In addition to the dream-writing material, I found that I spontaneously included a variety of my personal experiences and memories to flesh out the characters, setting, and plot. Is the story great? I had great fun writing it! Is there more of a story to tell? You bet!

As you practice intentional imagination and creative writing, begin with whatever inspires you from a dream and/or visionary meditation. As you write, your story will take on a life and form of its own. It is as if the creative impulse knows if it wants to take the form of a story or a poem or a piece of prose. Just let it happen.

PLAY WITH YOUR WORDS AND HAVE FUN!

One way to figure out the most appropriate form for your writing is to play around with developing the setting in which a particular activity in the dream took place. If the setting is particularly vivid, it will lend itself to further development. Of course, you also want to play with your characters and flesh them out. Take an emotion, an image, a motif, along with a character from a dream, and see what comes to you about an experience in the life of that character. Let the character speak to and through you. Follow his or her experience as you watch it unfold in that inner theater. Embellish the dream character from a fictional point of view as though you were writing a fictional biography or autobiography. In the process of elaborating the setting and the situation and fleshing out the characters, the story evolves into a more intricate plot. The story line naturally leads to some crisis or opportunity that, in turn, leads to a stalemate or a resolution. Your job is to let your imagination tell you what might happen next.

Many original dreams do not end with a resolution. It is your challenge to figure out the resolution as part of the fun and part of your individuation process. An unresolved dream story with strong emotional affect is a springboard for self-discovery and for prose and poetry writing.

Once you make an inner shift to support your intention to let the story or poem unfold, you are unconditionally free to follow your intentional imagination. Since this writing is no longer directly a reflection of the issue in your dream, you may write from a fictitious character's point of view, or an imaginary narrator's point of view.

Your style and voice will communicate an experience or idea effectively in a way that speaks to a particular audience. If that audience is limited to yourself, you will be writing yourself into being. You will be evolving yourself. And, if you happen to connect with readers who find what you write informative, that's part of the fun. As time and generations pass, what was once new news, becomes old news. Eventually old news once again becomes new news and bears restating.

When you catch sight of the images within your night world, take mental pictures, keep them safely stored in the photo album of your mind, and then write them into existence, you nourish your creative potential. As you strengthen your night wings by making repeated round trips to and from the source of your imagination, the visions you see transform into outer experiences. The shift from writing dreams to writing prose and poetry helps you develop a personal style and voice and use a variety of forms to express yourself in writing.

When you follow your dreams and express them creatively in your outer life, you expand the possibility and empower the probability that they will come true. You find the mentor, the guru, and storyteller within you as you reflect upon and give voice to the images and ideas in your dreams. Your creative impulse quickens as you give birth to all that is within you.

And why not?

APPENDIX:
STEPS OF SOULFUL
DREAM-WRITING PRACTICE

1. Record the dream in first-person present-tense fast-narrative style. (See chapter 3.)

2. What level is the dream? Why? (See chapter 2.)
    a. Personal
    b. Collective
    c. Transpersonal

3. What type of dream is it? Why? (See chapter 2.)
    a. Traumatic
    b. Compensatory
    c. Prospective:
    d. Extrasensory: telepathic or precognitive

4. What is your point of view in the dream? Why? (See chapter 4.)
    a. Participant
    b. Observer

5. Journal your associations to the setting, characters, plot, and emotions. (See chapter 4).

    a. *What do you feel* is the message of the dream? How and what did you feel, think, and identify with what was going on in the dream, the characters, the setting?

b. *Current Events:* what happened in the hours or the day just before the dream?

Associations: connections you sense between current events and the dream. What questions come up?

c. *Past Events:* what happened in the days, weeks, months, or years before the dream that pops up in your mind as you think about the dream? "That reminds me of . . ."

Associations: connections you sense between past events and the dream. What questions come up?

d. *Past Dreams:* what dreams have you had that contain similar elements?

Associations: connections you sense between past dreams and this dream. What questions come up?

6. Describe the shadow characters. (Female for woman; male for man. Review chapter 4.)

7. Describe the character and level of development for the anima— female images for a man—and the animus—male images for a woman. (See chapter 4.)

8. Describe the archetypes, i.e., the bigger-than-life characters. (See chapter 5.)

9. Write a visionary meditation with some aspect of the dream. (See chapter 6.)

10. Write prose or poetry that flows from the dream. (See chapter 7.)

NOTES

Chapter 1

1. C. G. Jung, *Two Essays on Analytical Psychology, The Collected Works of C. G. Jung* vol. 7, R.F.C. Hull, trans. Bollingen Series XX (Princeton: Princeton University Press, 1966), ¢ 234. Further references to the *Collected Works* will be cited as *CW*, with the volume number. Complete volume details are in the bibliography.
2. Jung, *CW* 9ii, ¢ 17.
3. Jung, *CW* 12, ¢ 175.
4. Jung, *CW* 10, ¢ 304.
5. Jung, *CW* 9ii, ¢ 257.

Chapter 2

1. Jung, *CW* 9i, ¢ 499.
2. Jung, *CW* 9i, ¢ 499.
3. C. G. Jung, *Memories, Dreams, Reflections.* Aniela Jaffé, ed. (New York: Pantheon Books, 1963), p. 273.
4. Jung, *CW* 8, ¢ 492.
5. Naomi Epel, *Writers Dreaming* (New York: Vintage Books, 1993), p. 26.
6. Jung, *CW* 8, ¢ 496.
7. Epel, *Writers Dreaming*, p. 240.
8. Jung, *CW* 8, ¢ 493.
9. Epel, *Writers Dreaming*, p. 134.
10. Jung, *CW* 9i, ¢ 396.
11. Jung, *CW* 15, ¢ 337.
12. Jung, *CW* 8, ¢ 973.
13. Epel, *Writers Dreaming*, p. 84.
14. Jung, *CW* 9i, ¢ 267.
15. Jung, *CW* 8, ¢ 506.
16. Jung, *CW* 6, ¢ 847.

Chapter 4

1. Jung, *CW* 9ii, ¢ 13.

Chapter 5

1. Jung, *CW* 7, ¢ 102.

2. Sogyal Rinpoche, *Glimpse After Glimpse: Daily Reflections on Living and Dying* (San Francisco: HarperSanFrancisco, 1995), January 14.

3. William James, *Varities of Religious Experience* (New York: Penguin Classics, 1982), p. 232.

4. Alberto Villoldo, *Shaman, Healer, Sage* (New York: Harmony Books, 2000), pp. 42–43.

5. Jung, *CW* 7, ¶ 46–47.

6. Jung, *CW* 8, ¶ 405.

7. James Hillman, *The Blue Fire: Selected Writings by James Hillman.* Thomas Moore, ed. (New York: Harper & Row, 1989), p. 23.

8. Several weeks after I finished writing this dream and my associations to it, I read William Anderson's *Green Man* (New York: Harper Collins, 1990), which associated the figure with the archetype of the serpent. Anderson observes that the Green Man first appeared at the end of a period that was characterized by a deep kinship with trees and woods. The symbol then adapted to the changing attitude toward nature brought about by the growth of Western science and technology. Anderson argues that the Green Man now signifies the coming together of the two modes of awareness in a new experience of conscious participation.

9. Anderson, *Green Man*, p. 164.

10. Jung, *CW* 7, ¶ 118.

11. Jung, *CW* 9i, ¶ 248.

12. Jung, *CW* 7, ¶ 118.

13. Sogyal Rinpoche, *Glimpse after Glimpse*, February 28.

14. Jung, *CW* 18, ¶ 554.

15. Marie-Louise von Franz, "The Process of Individuation," in C. G. Jung, ed., *Man and His Symbols* (New York: Doubleday, 1969) pp. 195, 206.

16. John Sanford's book, *The Invisible Partners* (New Jersey: Paulist Press, 1989) provides an excellent way to become more familiar with these aspects of the unconscious dream figures.

17. Jung, *CW* 9i, ¶ 393.

Chapter 6

1. Jung, *CW* 9i, ¶ 399.

2. James Hollis, *Archetypal Imagination*, (College Station, TX: Texas A&M University Press, 2000), p. 48.

3. Barbara Hannah, *Encounters with the Soul: Active Imagination* (Santa Monica, CA: Sigo Press, 1981), p. 57.

4. Jung, *CW* 7, ¶ 159.

5. Carlos Castaneda, *The Art of Dreaming* (New York: Harper Collins, 1993), p. 21.

6. Jung, *CW* 10, ¶ 304.

7. Castaneda, *Art of Dreaming*, p. 29.

8. Alberto Villoldo and Erik Jendresen, *Island of the Sun: Mastering the Inca Medicine Wheel* (Rochester, VT: Destiny Books, 1995), p. 208.

9. Jung, *CW* 7, ¶ 230.

10. Hannah, *Encounters with the Soul*, p. 17.

11. In Doris Lessing's novel, *The Golden Notebook* (Toronto: Bantam, 1973), she gives the competing parts of the main character's psyche separate journals in which to write, because "she rec-

ognizes she has to separate things off from each other, out of fear of chaos, of a formless-ness—of breakdown" (p. vii).

12. Jung, *CW* 11, ⟨ 53.

Chapter 7

1. Jung, *CW* 11, ⟨ 875.
2. Jung, *CW* 8, ⟨ 5.
3. Jung, *CW* 15, ⟨ 143.
4. Jung, *CW* 15, ⟨ 15.
5. Jung, *CW* 7, ⟨ 344.
6. C. G. Jung, *Letters* vol. I (Princeton: Princeton University Press, 1973), pp. 458–461.
7. Jung, *Letters* vol. I, pp. 458–461.
8. Jung, *CW* 8, ⟨ 186.
9. C. G. Jung, *Memories, Dreams, Reflections*, Aniela Jaffé, ed. (New York: Vintage, 1965), p. 178.
10. Clive Barker, *Galilee* (New York: HarperCollins, 1999), p. 606.

Chapter 8

1. Naomi Epel, *Writers Dreaming* (New York: Vintage Books, 1993), p. 96.
2. David Feinstein and Stanley Krippner, *The Mythic Path* (New York: Jeremy P. Tarcher, 1997), p. 3.
3. Jung, *CW* 15, ⟨ 337.

BIBLIOGRAPHY

Anderson, William. *Green Man.* New York: Harper Collins, 1990.

Barker, Clive. *Galilee.* New York: Harper Collins, 1999.

Castaneda, Carlos. *The Art of Dreaming.* New York: Harper Collins, 1993.

Epel, Naomi. *Writers Dreaming.* New York: Vintage Books, 1993.

Edinger, Edward. "Notes on Analytical Psychology." In *Quadrant,* 1968.

Feinstein, David and Stanley Krippner. *The Mythic Path.* New York: Jeremy P. Tarcher, 1997.

Fitzgerald, F. Scott. *The Crack Up.* New York: Penguin Books, 1965.

Hannah, Barbara. *Encounters with the Soul: Active Imagination.* Santa Monica, CA: Sigo Press, 1981.

Hillman, James. *The Blue Fire: Selected Writings by James Hillman.* Edited by Thomas Moore. New York: Harper & Row, 1989.

Hollis, James. *Archetypal Imagination.* College Station, TX: Texas A&M University Press, 2000.

James, William. *Varities of Religious Experience.* New York: Penguin Classics, 1982.

Jung, C. G. *Aion: Researches into the Phenomenology of the Self, The Collected Works of C. G. Jung* vol. 9ii. R.F.C. Hull, trans., Bollingen Series XX. Princeton: Princeton University Press, 1969.

———. *The Archetypes and the Collective Unconscious, The Collected Works of C. G. Jung* vol. 9i. R.F.C. Hull, trans. Bollingen Series XX. Princeton: Princeton University Press, 1969.

―――――. *Civilization in Transition, The Collected Works of C. G. Jung* vol. 10. R.F.C. Hull, trans., Bollingen Series XX. Princeton: Princeton University Press, 1970.

―――――. *Dream Analysis: Notes of the Seminar.* Edited by William McGuire. Princeton: Princeton University Press, 1984.

―――――. *Letters.* 2 vols. Princeton, NJ: Princeton University Press, 1973.

―――――. *Memories, Dreams & Reflections.* Edited by Aniela Jaffé. New York: Vintage, 1965.

―――――. *Psychological Reflections.* Edited by Jolande Jacobi. New York: Harper Torchbook, 1961.

―――――. *Psychological Types, The Collected Works of C. G. Jung* vol. 6. R.F.C. Hull, trans. Bollingen Series XX. Princeton: Princeton University Press, 1976.

―――――. *Psychology and Alchemy, The Collected Works of C. G. Jung* vol. 12. R.F.C. Hull, trans. Bollingen Series XX. Princeton: Princeton University Press, 1980.

―――――. *Psychology and Religion: West and East, The Collected Works of C.G. Jung* vol. 11. R.F.C. Hull, trans. Bollingen Series XX. Princeton: Princeton University Press, 1970.

―――――. *The Structure and Dynamics of the Psyche, The Collected Works of C. G. Jung* vol. 8. R.F.C. Hull, trans., Bollingen Series XX. Princeton: Princeton University Press, 1970.

―――――. *The Spirit in Man, Art & Literature, The Collected Works of C. G. Jung* vol. 15. R.F.C. Hull, trans. Bollingen Series XX. Princeton: Princeton University Press, 1966.

―――――. *The Symbolic Life: Miscellaneous Writings. The Collected Works of C. G. Jung* vol. 18. R.F.C. Hull, trans. Bollingen Series XX. Princeton: Princeton University Press, 1977.

————. *Two Essays on Analytical Psychology, The Collected Works of C. G. Jung* vol. 7. R.F.C. Hull, trans. Bollingen Series XX. Princeton: Princeton University Press, 1966.

Jung, C. G., ed. *Man & His Symbols.* New York: Doubleday, 1969.

Lessing, Doris. *The Golden Notebook.* Toronto: Bantam, 1973.

Morton, Chris and Ceri Louise Thomas, *The Mystery of the Crystal Skulls.* New York: HarperCollins,1998.

Perera, Sylvia B. *Descent to the Goddess.* Toronto: Inner City Books, 1981.

Sanford, John. *The Invisible Partners.* New Jersey: Paulist Press, 1989.

————. *The Kingdom Within: The Inner Meaning of Jesus' Sayings.* New York: Harper & Row, 1987.

Sogyal Rinpoche. *Glimpse after Glimpse: Daily Reflections on Living and Dying.* San Francisco: HarperSanFrancisco, 1995.

Villoldo, Alberto, *Shaman, Healer, Sage.* New York: Harmony Books, 2000.

————. *The Four Winds Newsletter.* 2001.

Villoldo, Alberto and Erik Jendresen. *Island of the Sun: Mastering the Inca Medicine Wheel.* Rochester, VT: Destiny Books, 1995.

Washburn, Michael. *The Ego and the Dynamic Ground: Transpersonal Theory of Human Development.* Albany: State University of New York Press, 1988.

INDEX

active imagination, 62, 117, 134

alchemy, 16

algebra dream, 57

Angelou, Maya, 23

anger, 127

anima, 84, 107

animus, 84, 107; negative, 84–85

antagonists, 73, 79–80; archetypal, 105–106; collective/transpersonal, 106; personal, 106

archetypes, 7–8, 105; anima, 107–110; animus, 107–110; Dream Work with (exercise), 106–107; as mentors, 97–105; role in dream, example of, 98–99; serpent, 114–115; spiritual, 114; transpersonal, 8, antagonistic, example of, 109–110; *Art of Dreaming, The*, 43

associations, 67; to a Dream (exercise), 90–91

attention, first, 43; second, 43, 44, 123, directing, 123–125

Australian aborigines, 2

awareness, extraordinary, 14–15

Barker, Clive, 169

Brasan Feasa, 102

Breathing and Centering Meditation (exercise), 49–50

breathing meditation, 48–50; physical sensations of, 47–48

Buddha, 2

car dream, 24–25

Castaneda, Carlos, 43

centering, 48–50

chakra centers, 16

characters, 33–34, 75–87; Antagonistic

Anima and Animus (exercise), 86; Antagonistic Shadow (exercise), 81; archetypal, 158; dialogue with, 161–162; fleshing out, 156–159, example of, 176, transpersonal, 160–164; Personal Dream, Developing (exercise), 158–159; shadow, 6; Transpersonal Dream, Developing Your (exercise), 163

chi, 16

cognitive behavior model of personality, 84

Collected Works of C. G. Jung, xii

collective dreams, 1, 20–21, 91, 93–94, 101, 102, 105, 107, 160, 105, 170; *see also dreams*

collective setting, 72, 73

collective unconscious, 1, 3, 4, 6–7, 27, 29, 53, 67, 84, 86, 93–94, 96, 100, 101, 106, 111, 114, 116, 122, 143, 175

complex, 121–122

conflict, unresolved, 131–132

consciousness, altered states of, 43

Creative Writing (exercise), 152–153

creativity, 40

critic, inner, 135–137; (exercise), 136

deflation, 76

denial, 133

depth psychology, 4

dramatic structure, 151

dream, anger in, 127; analysis, 21; bigger-than-life, 76; catchers, 43; dictionaries, 67; ego, 70, 73, as protagonist, 78–79, 105; erotic, 126; fearful, 126; gaining insight into, 115–116; interpretation books, 118; joyful, 126; Living with